Sephari

THE SCIENCE OF NUMEROLOGY

To Moya,

Happy Birthday

Love

Kate.
xx

METAPHYSICAL MATHEMATICS

Sepharial's
THE SCIENCE OF NUMEROLOGY

Author of
"The Kabala of Numbers"

LONDON
W. Foulsham & CO. LTD.
NEW YORK - TORONTO - CAPE TOWN - SYDNEY

W. FOULSHAM & CO. LTD.
Yeovil Road, Slough, Berks, England.

ISBN 0-572-01436-8

© *W. Foulsham & Co. Ltd. 1987*

Made and printed in Great Britain by
St Edmundsbury Press Ltd, Bury St Edmunds, Suffolk

PREFACE

Numerology is a science which has survived the test of thousands of years. The learned Ancients discovered the co-relationship of numbers, the planetary influences over life on this earth and the ordered planning of the universe.

In modern times, no one has made a greater study of this science than Sepharial. His earlier works on the subject were closely allied to Astrology but the present volume is written so that those without any astrological knowledge may have a clear exposition of numerology in every aspect of daily life.

CONTENTS

Chapter		Page
I	The Mysticism of Numbers	9
II	The Hebrew Kabala	22
III	Names and Numbers	31
IV	Numbers and Character	40
V	Your Love and Marriage Number	56
VI	Your Lucky and Money Numbers	76
VII	Your Number of Health	96
VIII	Colour and Numbers	111
IX	Numbers and Speculation	116
	Football Pools	117
	Stocks and Shares	121
	Horse and Greyhound Racing	125

CHAPTER ONE

THE MYSTICISM OF NUMBERS

The philosophers of ancient Greece believed that numbers possessed some mysterious power independent of their arithmetical significance.

Thomas Taylor in his translation of Iamblicus' *Life of Pythagoras* said: "The Pythagoreans received from the theology of Orpheus the principles of intelligible and intellectual numbers; they assigned them an abundant progression, and extended their dominion."

Hence that proverb was peculiar to the Pythagoreans that all things are assimilated to numbers. Pythagoras, therefore, in the *Sacred Discourse* clearly stated: "Number is the ruler of forms and ideas, and is the cause of gods and demons."

Numbers are used to express quantitative values in relation to Unity, which of itself is the first expression of Zero. From Zero all numbers proceed and into Zero they all are resolved again. Thus it comes about that the digits from first to last are represented by the number 10, the Alpha and

Omega of all enumeration. If we set out the digits in their order we find that they present to us a very curious set of relations, thus:

1 2 3 4 5 6 7 8 9.

Bringing the first and last of these series together in order successively, we have—

> 1 and 9 equals 10,
> 2 and 8 equals 10,
> 3 and 7 equals 10,
> 4 and 6 equals 10,

leaving behind the characteristic number 5, which represents the human species with its five avenues of sensation, its five digits or fingers, its five peduncles or toes, and its five great Races. This number was held in great veneration by the ancients, and we find that among the Chinese and among the Hindus there is a tendency to count by fives. Thus the Chinese have the Wu hing or five useful things, the five precepts of conduct, five ranks of office, five kinds of punishment, etc. The five useful things were clay, wood, metal, fire and water. These were ruled by five planets.

> Saturn ruled earth or clay.
> Jupiter ruled wood.
> Venus ruled metal.
> Mars ruled fire.
> Mercury ruled water

So they called the names of the planets the Earth Star, the Wood Star, the Metal Star, and so on. The five precepts were filial love, loyalty, marital fidelity, obedience and sincerity, as regulating the relations between parents and their children, the rulers and the people, husbands and wives, masters and servants, man and friend. The five sorts of punishment were by fines, the rod, the scourge, banishment, and death.

Thus five may be said to stand for humanity and for human relations, man standing as it were in the middle ground of the manifest and unmanifest worlds, and in a measure cognising both the material and immaterial worlds by sense and thought, himself being the embodiment of all, an epitome of the universe, a veritable microcosm.

> The total of the digits 1 to 9 is 45, or nine times 5.
>
> The total of the odd numbers is 25, or five times 5.
>
> The total of the even numbers is 20, or four times 5.

But each of the numbers comprised in the series has its traditional value as a symbol, and these symbols are associated with the Sun and members of the Solar system.

Note: This series is the astrological series or unit system which should not be confused with the Kabalistic series based on the Hebrew alphabet of twenty-two letters, which is described in Chapter 2.

In the Astrological series or unit system the symbol

ONE

is the symbol of the manifest Deity, who came

forth from the Abyss of Nothingness, or Infinitude. It is the symbol of the Sun, the light that shone in the darkness of the world's great night and became the source of all revelation, of heat and light, of wisdom and love, the vortex centre of the universe of worlds, the archetype. Hence it is symbolised as a circle with a point in the centre. Thus: ☉

It is the beginning; that by which all the rest of the nine numbers are created. The basis of all numbers is ONE; the basis of all life is ONE. This number represents all that is creative, individual and positive. It stands for force, boldness and activity as well as for powers of organising and executive ability.

Two

is the symbol of relativity, antithesis, witness, and confirmation. It denotes the binomial and "pairs of opposites," as positive and negative, active and passive, male and female, light and dark, etc., in relation to Unity, which stands for the first named of these, two standing for the second of them. It represents the dualism of manifested life, as God and Nature, Spirit and Matter, Osiris and Isis, and their interrelations. It denotes the Law of Alternation in natural operations. It embodies the idea of procreation, fruition, combination, relationship of opposites, the two conditions: manifest and unmanifest; the explicit and implicit; buying and selling. It is symbolised by the Moon:☽.

The Moon is related to two numbers, of which the number "2" gives the negative vibration. This can be understood as being the position when the Moon is in conjunction with the sun, *i.e.* New Moon, and the Moon throwing no reflected light upon the earth. This number denotes relativity, vacillation and change.

The Moon also stands for form and the growth of form and is the female counterpart of Number One, the two together creating the third number.

THREE

is the trilogy of Life, Substance and Intelligence, applicable to the Divine BEING; of Force, Matter, and Consciousness, applicable to natural EXISTENCE. Creation, preservation and resolution. Father, mother and child—Osiris, Isis and Horus—God, Nature and Man. The three dimensions of space. The three postulates—thought, the thinker and the thing. The three parts of Time—past, present and future. Thus it denotes in itself the idea of extension in both time and space, and stands for penetration, procedure and pervasion. It is symbolised by the planet Jupiter, a planet which plays a most important role both in astrology and in all systems of numerology. It is the beginning of what may be termed one of the main lines of force that runs right through all the numbers from one to nine. It has a special relation to every third number in the series such as three, six, nine. These numbers added together in any direction produce a nine as their final digit.

$$3 + 6 + 9 = 18 = 9$$
$$6 + 9 + 3 = 18 = 9$$
$$9 + 3 + 6 = 18 = 9$$

Total of each column 18 18 18 54 27
reduced to unit = 9 9 9 9 9

The number also stands for inclusion, comprehension, understanding, judgment; for increase, fecundity and propagation; thus and for self-expansion, the harvesting of the fruits of action, reward, equity, justice. Reproduction in the material world. Fatherhood, familism. By extension of self it becomes a symbol of sympathy, benevolence, charity, philanthropy, etc., and, by reflection, of joy, good fortune, and plenty. It is denoted by the planet Jupiter: ♃

FOUR

is the number of reality and concretion. Solids, the cube or square, the cross. Physical laws, logic, reason. Appearance, physiognomy, science, cognition. Segmentation, partition, order, classification. The Wheel of Fortune, the Wheel of Ixion, the Wheel of the Law, sequence, enumeration. The intellect which discerns between the noumenal and phenomenal, thought and perception. Discernment, discretion, relativity. It is symbolised by the Sun, ☉, of which it is the negative number. Being a negative number it is, therefore, formative instead of creative as with the number One. It shows a sequence of organic changes. It is a number which is associated with alchemical processes involving sublimation and transmutation and all mutation of atomic structure, ancient or modern.

This is also the number of opposition, rebellion and explosion and, in the latter, may be likened to the principle of chain re-action and thus links with the modern scientific trend of nuclear fission.

FIVE

is the number of variety, adaptability and mental change. It has rule over the outer consciousness which deals with the material factors of life and the process of discrimination, analysis, sometimes the tearing of things to pieces as in criticism. All forms of literary expression and the exercise of local government come under its vibration. It is symbolised by the planet Mercury: ☿.

In its constructive aspect it gives a wonderful elasticity of thought and inspiration which can be expressed in speech and writing thus making oratory and the written word key-notes of the number's influence. From the less favourable angle the vibration brings a danger of active plagiarism. Vacillation and indicision are concomitant factors and if given way to will weaken the character and cause ultimate loss of prestige and reputation. The number is associated with quicksilver, the volatile qualities of which are well known, as it can split into a myriad particles in a moment of time and yet coalesce again just as quickly.

The number often expresses itself in a dual capacity, drawing out the potential for both good and evil, ranging from the highest intellectual attainment to the lowest degree of mental debasement.

Six

is the number of co-operation, of marriage, interlacing, link or connection. It represents the two triads in their interaction, the Seal of Solomon* or interlaced triangles. The interplay of spirit and matter, the human soul; psychology, divination, communion, psychism, telepathy, spychometry, and alchemy. The Great Work. Co-ordination, concord, harmony, peace, satisfaction, happiness and material well-being. Intercourse and reciprocity. Connubiality, the relations of the sexes. It is indicated by the planet Venus: ♀.

In certain instances the number Six is considered a rather weak number, and its weakness is intensified in terms of human character and destiny if more than one Six appears in the computation of the name-number or the number horoscope. Readers will recall references which have been made in biblical and other writings to the beastiality of the number 6 6 6 which is really three sixes and is termed the number of the "Beast". When two or more sixes occur the principle of temptation becomes emphasised and exercises a malign influence over life and destiny.

* See *The Book of Charms and Talismans*

Seven

governs the cyclic law of time. The breaking back of the natural to the spiritual; liberation; revolution; reaction, separation. It is emblematic of the seven ages of man, the seven days of the week, the seven seals, the seven notes of the musical scale, and the seven prismatic colours—Violet, Indigo, Blue, Green, Yellow, Orange and Red. It is symbolised by the Moon, ☽, of which it is the positive number. In this positive expression it is associated with the full Moon when the Moon is in exact opposition to the Sun and thus reflecting the full light of the Sun onto the Earth.

Seven is the mystical number, the number which governs all rites and ceremonies of a magical nature which can only be performed correctly at the time of the full moon. The invoking of elemental forces and spirits, the performing of exorcism for the banishment of evil spirits, the overcoming of obsessions and the forcing of a discontinuance of poltergeist phenomena are all the more easily performed by using the number seven in the ritualistic preparation, particularly at the time of the full Moon.

This number is greatly associated with the domestic and family conditions of life and has much to do with the function of childbirth, which is the actual delivery of the infant and the commencement of a separate existence.

Eight

is the number of completion. Time and space, duration and distance, old age, decadence and death.

There are many curious things in history as regards this number. The Greeks called it the number of Justice on account of its equal divisions of equally even numbers. The Jews practised circumcision on the eighth day after birth. At their Feast of Dedication they kept eight candles burning and their Feast lasted eight days. Eight prophets were descended from Rahab. There were eight sects of Pharisees. Noah was the eighth in direct descent from Adam. The strange number of three eights (8 8 8) is considered by certain students of occultism to be the number of Jesus Christ in His aspect as the redeemer of the world. This number 8 8 8 given to Christ is in direct opposition to 6 6 6 which the Book of Revelations states is "the number of the Beast or the number of Man." It is symbolised by the planet Saturn: ♄. From the earliest ages it has been associated with the symbol of an irrevocable Fate both in the lives of individuals and with Nations. It may be pointed out that the planet Saturn is the ruling planet of the Jewish race, a race which has felt the hand of Fate through the centuries. On the other hand, the number eight and the planet Saturn are both associated with destiny which is, in essence, the higher attribute of Fate, as it gives the individual the freedom of action which can be creative of either Destiny of Fate.

NINE

is the number of activity, energy, the fighter, the battle, the element of strife, and the expressing of courage. It shows a danger of foolhardiness, of impulsiveness of word and action, of quarrels and strife, and of accidents, particularly from fire and explosion. Resourcefulness and capacity for organisation whether it be applied to the exigencies of the battlefield or the vocational interests of life, are common assets of this number. It is symbolised by the planet Mars: ♂.

The number nine has some curious properties. In mathematics it is the only number that, multiplied by any other number, always reproduces itself. For example, 9 times seven is 63, and 6 plus 3 once again becomes 9. *This is the case with every number that it is multiplied by.*

It is also of interest to note that in ancient burials the dead were always buried on the ninth day. The Saviour died at the ninth hour. Both the first and second temples of the Jews were destroyed on the ninth day of the Jewish month called Ab. In comparatively recent times the planetary scale was advanced from seven to nine by the discovery (or re-discovery) of the planets Uranus and Neptune, the former being discovered in the 18th century (9) and the latter in the next century, *i.e.* 1845 (9).

There is again a mysterious association of the

number 9 with the number 6 6 6 for, if these three sixes are added together, 18 is obtained and 1 plus 8 gives the figure 9. This is really the spiritual number of 6 6 6.

ZERO (0)

stands for Eternity, immensity, the infinite, infinitude, the universe in concept, Divine conception, ideation universality, circumambulation, navigation, circulation. Also for circumference, limitation, privation, restriction, and imperfection. Thus it is the universal paradox, the infinitely great and the infinitely small, Boundless Being and the Atom. Its symbol is the planet Pluto: P.

The cipher (0) is associated with the repetitive principle for, when it is added to 1, it becomes ten and when doubly added becomes 100, and so on. Thus it shows transformation and the long term plan of action. It can also signify negation. It has rule over atomic power or force and, from the standpoint of human character or destiny, it will rule the unknown or unseen factor which is often referred to as the "X" factor.

In the 20th century the planetary scale was stepped up to 10 by the discovery of the planet Pluto. It is interesting to note that both the planetary scale and the century involved have had the cipher "0" amplified. This planet has definite rule over the Atom and the "H" bomb, which have both been developed since the discovery of Pluto, and whose function of annihilation is one of the attributes of this planet.

These ascriptions follow the order of the days of the week and the Hebraic system of planetary numbers, thus:—

0 Space, Pluto; 1 and 4 the Sun (1 positive, 4 negative); 2 and 7 the Moon (2 negative, 7 positive); 3 Jupiter; 5 Mercury; 6 Venus; 8 Saturn; 9 Mars.

The corresponding days are: 1 and 4, Sunday; 2 and 7, Monday; 9, Tuesday; 5, Wednesday; 3, Thursday; 6, Friday; 8, Saturday.

The planets Uranus, Neptune and Pluto do not come within the ordinary septenary scale as they commence the second octave of planetary vibrations. Uranus, however, being the octave of Mercury, will be associated in its positive aspect with Wednesday and the number 5, and in its negative aspect, with Sunday, number 4 and the Sun. The reason for this is that Uranus is the secondary ruler of the sign Aquarius, the opposition sign to Leo which is ruled by the Sun. In the case of Neptune, which is the octave of Venus, it will in its positive aspect be associated with Friday and the number 6, but in its negative aspect it interchanges with the Moon and thus will influence Monday and the number 2. Pluto is the octave expression of Mars and from its positive standpoint will influence Tuesday and the number 8; its negative side is the cipher 0.

CHAPTER TWO

THE HEBREW KABALA

In the previous chapter a description has been given of what may be termed the single or "unit" numbers from 1 to 9 and of the Cipher "0", together with correspondences to the Sun, Moon and planets, and the days of the week.

There is, however, an extension of number allocation beyond the unit bringing in what may be termed double or composite numbers from 10 to 22. This extension is associated with the Hebrew Kabala. The word Kabala means Traditional Knowledge.

In the Hebrew Alphabet there are 22 letters and these are linked with the numbers from 1 to 22, and with the letters of the English Alphabet. As the latter consists of 26 letters there are in certain instances a grouping of more than one English letter for the corresponding Hebrew letter. The following Table shows the Hebrew letter, the English Equivalent and the associated number together with the zodiacal or planetary ruler.

Hebrew Letter	English Letter	Number	Planetary or Zodiacal Ruler
Aleph	A	1	☿ Mercury
Beth	B	2	♍ Virgo
Gimel	G	3	♎ Libra
Daleth	D	4	♏ Scorpio
He	E	5	♃ Jupiter
Vau	V U W	6	♀ Venus
Zain	Z	7	♐ Sagittarius
Cheth	H	8	♑ Capricorn
Teth	Th	9	♒ Aquarius
Jod	I J Y	10	♅ Uranus
Caph	C K	11	♆ Neptune
Lamed	L	12	♓ Pisces
Mem	M	13	♈ Aries
Nun	N	14	♉ Taurus
Sameck	X	15	♄ Saturn
Ayin	O	16	♂ Mars
Pe	F P	17	♊ Gemini
Tzaddi	Ts Tz	18	♋ Cancer
Quoph	Q	19	♌ Leo
Resh	R	20	☽ Moon
Shin	S	21	☉ Sun
Tau	T	22	⊕ Earth

With the number 10 as an integral number we come to the first of the double numbers and these each have a distinctive influence.

The number TEN in itself shows a transition from the units to the double numbers and therefore denotes a change and a manifesting of vibrations and conditions upon another and a different plane, of spirituality, of mentality or thought, and of physical action or material expression. Whereas the number ONE came under the influence of Mercury, the ruler of the brain and the mind, the number TEN comes under the influence of the planet Uranus which is the octave expression of Mercury and governs the twin factors of Inspiration and Genius. Mercury rules the literary processes of thought, Uranus rules the scientific and, in its influence over the life and destiny of the individual, will bring sudden and unexpected changes of thought and action and of Fortune, sometimes for good and sometimes for ill, sometimes as a result of the volitional thought and action of the individual, at other times as a direct result of Fate, or circumstance.

The number ELEVEN operates through the higher emotional side of the nature, showing the expression of universal compassion and love as distinct from the personal and selfish form of love which is often based upon passion. It is a feminine and a magnetic number and has a great deal to do with psychic force as well as spiritual power and fortitude. It comes under the domination of the planet Neptune and gives the capacity to use the power of suggestion so as to influence other people and help them in the overcoming of physical, moral and spiritual weakness.

The number TWELVE is also an emotional number giving a superb understanding of the depths of human emotion and suffering. As a result of this understanding it gives the capacity to make sacrifices for others and to "turn the other cheek" when abused or ill-treated. Despite all the vicissitudes of life there will be a warmness of expression towards other people and a maintaining of a sense of humour. Responding to the vibration of the zodiacal sign of Pisces it arouses the desire to heal the sick. It is the number of Nursing and of Administration.

The number THIRTEEN is another number of transformation, this time having rule over matters to do with both life and death and the transition from the earthly to the astral sphere of activity. It signifies the beginning of a new cycle where there is more freedom and where the thraldom of the material and financial cares of earthly life are absent. From another angle it is the number of bravery and of the pioneer, for it responds to the influence of the Zodiacal sign Aries. It draws out a natural degree of the kind of courage needed to handle the varying fluctuations in ordinary life and to face up to danger and even to death when they occur.

The number FOURTEEN is a more material and physical number. It has to do with Nature itself and with what may be termed the Forces of Nature. It is a conserving number and yet has extreemly great potentiality of power when it is unleashed. To some extent it is associated with the factor of growth—the growth of living organisms—and with beauty, art, music and singing, whilst from a more material standpoint it will have influence over money and over precious stones in their entirety. The zodiacal sign of Taurus exercises its sway over this number, giving firmness, inertia or obstinacy and yet dynamic force that will not be frustrated.

The number FIFTEEN is the number of Fate and of Destiny. It gives Power and yet can take it away. In some respects it is a number of mystery and of matters to do with the Underworld, of Purgatory or Hell, where the soul of the individual may languish as a result of evil things done whilst on earth. It warns that the exercise of authority should never be abused, for it is also a number associated with the principle of Justice. As one sows so must one reap. It is dominated by the planet Saturn. It shows that, if power is used wrongly, a fall from position must occur and a Karma is created for future earthly incarnation; but if power is used justly and wisely, then the principle of Predestination becomes operative.

The number SIXTEEN is another very powerful number, both for good and for ill. It governs the physical forces and passions, blind anger, rash impulse, temper, and yet, from the constructive standpoint, shows the capacity to be aggressive when there is the necessity to put up a fight against wrong-doing and the evil actions and brutality of others. It can bring a spirit of rivalry and, when this is permitted unduly, it can cause destruction; but when used to promote healthy competition for constructive ends, it will give tremendous force and energy. It is ruled by the planet Mars, the planet of war and pestilence but also the planet of exploration and discovery.

The number SEVENTEEN is another spiritual number and expresses the principle of Immortality, the continuity of life in its various forms and phases, the continuity of ideas and of principles themselves. Some of these principles can be summarised as Truth, Hope, Faith, Charity, principles that persist through all ages and are to be found in all races and in all parts of the world. It is a number of illumination and aids in the understanding of life, of science and of destiny. It is influenced by the Zodiacal sign of Gemini, representative of intellectual force, of intuition and of reason.

The number EIGHTEEN is what may be termed a "difficult" number. It shows an attack by the materialistic side of the nature on the spiritual attributes. There is a danger of giving way to intrigue and deception on the one hand and of encountering false friends and secret foes on the other hand. It gives a warning of both treachery and danger, causes bitter quarrels which can involve friends and family and implies periods of danger through water, fires and even explosions. Astrologically it is influenced by the sign Cancer which, although giving a tenacity of purpose, can also bring a fear of the unknown.

The number NINETEEN on the other hand is one

of the fortunate numbers. It brings conditions of happiness and joy, and is especially helpful and favourable for all interests to do with children and young people. It is one of the creative numbers, physically, mentally and emotionally, and is significator of such love as springs unselfishly into manifestation as a result of natural harmony and of joy of life. It will bring much progress, advancement and attainment, and as it is under the vibration of the Zodiacal sign of Leo with the pictorial symbol of the Sun, it is a number promising success, honour and esteem.

The number TWENTY is again a mainly favourable number, although its fortune depends to a great extent upon the Faith, and Effort, of the individual. It symbolises Awakening or Resurrection, and from a spiritual standpoint shows that there must be a firm faith that there is an after life and a continuation of activity after the death of the physical body, if spiritual progress is to be made and inner understanding and illumination obtained. Similarly there must be faith in the individual ability to do things as well as a putting forth of personal effort in order to demonstrate that ability and thus bring about progress along that particular sphere of life which is of greatest interest. The Moon is the planetary ruler of this number and it governs the principle of gestation.

The number TWENTY-ONE is a number of advancement and of elevation. It shows the crowning factor of achievement as a result of effort—

the obtaining of power, of authority, of recognition. It will bring victory after a long fight. It symbolises the one who is at the head of affairs irrespective of whether they are spiritual or material. It is the number of the Adept, the King, the President, the Head of the Clan, Cause or Home. It comes under the vibration of the Sun as the planetary ruler and shows a working out of Destiny in a positive manner.

The number TWENTY-TWO is an unfortunate number. It is the number that inspires doubt and unbelief and shows an individual who is in danger of letting his own conceit and vanity blind him to the spiritual, emotional and physical dangers that beset his path. It is a number warning against illusion and delusion, a number of false judgment and degeneration unless the individual awakens to the realisation of its weakness. If so, then the liability to failure, folly or mistake can be overcome. It is under the rulership of the Earth and as such does intensify the dogma of materialism, sometimes of atheism and of the negation of spiritual virtues; but it shows that the lessons of life can bring about a breaking of the bonds which limit and restrict the consciousness and, once this occurs, the materialist vibration is overcome.

The interpretation of a number can be based on either the unit system or the Kabala; but in order to avoid confusion it must be stated that, in the unit system, only the planetary influence is used and no reference is made to the signs of the Zodiac. The letters of the English Alphabet and their corresponding number and planetary vibration are given in the table below.

UNIT SYSTEM

Letter	Number	Planetary Influence
A I J Q Y	1	☉ Sun positive
B C K R	2	☽ Moon negative
G L S	3	♃ Jupiter
D M T	4	☉ Sun negative
E N	5	☿ Mercury
U V W	6	♀ Venus
O X Z	7	☽ Moon positive
H F P	8	♄ Saturn
Th Ts Tz	9	♂ Mars

NOTE: In the Unit System there is no influence from the planets Uranus, Neptune, Pluto.

CHAPTER THREE

NAMES AND NUMBERS

In unlocking the meaning of a name, the numerical value of that name must first be obtained by the adding together of the numbers that correspond to each letter of the name, finding the sum total and then either reducing this to a unit, *i.e.* 1 to 9, if the unit system of numbers is used, or reducing to number 22 or under should the Kabalistic system of numbers be used; for, as already explained, each of the 22 numbers associated with the Kabala has a specific influence.

Let us, therefore, take a few examples at first of Christian or Forenames—not surnames, as they describe family traits and family history rather than the personal or individual character and fortune.

A few popular names will serve to show the method involved and both the Unit and Hebrew Kabalistic system of numbers will be illustrated:

Unit System	*Kabala*
A R T H U R	A R T H U R
1 2 4 8 6 2	1 20 22 8 6 20
= 23 = 5	= 77 = 14

Here we see that the unit system of numbering brings in the influence of the number 5 whilst the Kabala brings in the influence of the number 14. With the Unit system the number 5 is ruled by Mercury whereas in the Kabala the number 14 brings in the influence of the sign Taurus. If one wishes to take a composite or extremely broad view of the character then both descriptions could be taken and applied, the description of Mercury being found under the number 1 on page 41, and the description of Taurus and the number 14 being found on page 49 in chapter 4.

Further illustrations of names:—

Unit System	*Kabala*
E D W A R D	E D W A R D
5 4 6 1 2 4	5 4 6 1 20 4
= 22 = 4	= 40 = 4

In this instance the final result of the number comes to the same, 4 in each case, and when this occurs it can be taken as a concentrating or consolidating of the particular vibration of that number on the character. The number 4 brings in the influence of the Zodiacal sign of Scorpio which will be found on page 43, Chapter 4.

Unit System	*Kabala*
S I D N E Y	S I D N E Y
3 1 4 5 5 1	22 10 4 14 5 10
= 19 = 10 = 1	= 65 = 11

There are again two numbers involved and the number 1 in the Unit System brings in the in-

NAMES AND NUMBERS

fluence of the Sun positive which will be found on page 54 of Chapter 4 whilst the number 11 brings in the influence of Neptune, to be found on page 47 in that chapter.

Unit System	*Kabala*
G E O R G E	G E O R G E
3 5 7 2 3 5	3 5 16 20 3 5
= 25 = 7	= 52 = 7

Both numbers are the same, the influence of 7 in the Unit system being the positive number of the Moon, the description is given by the Moon, Chapter 4, page 53. In the Kabala 7 brings in the influence of the sign Sagittarius, Chapter 4, page 44.

Unit System	*Kabala*
A L F R E D	A L F R E D
1 3 8 2 5 4	1 12 17 20 5 4
= 23 = 5	= 59 = 14

In the Unit system the number 5 brings in the influence of the planet Mercury, Chapter 4, page 41 whilst the Kabala brings in the influence of the sign Taurus, Chapter 4, page 49.

Unit System	*Kabala*
H E R B E R T	H E R B E R T
8 5 2 2 5 2 4	8 5 20 2 5 20 22
= 28 = 10 = 1	= 82 = 10

The number 1 in the Unit system brings in the influence of the Sun (positive), Chapter 4, page 54 whilst the number 10 of the Kabala brings in the influence of the planet Uranus, Chapter 4, page 47.

Unit System   *Kabala*
J O H N   J O H N
1 7 8 5   10 16 8 14
= 21 = 3   = 48 = 12

The number 3 in the Unit system shows the influence of the planet Jupiter, Chapter 4, page 43 whilst the number 12 in the Kabala shows the influence of the sign Pisces, Chapter 4, page 48.

Unit System   *Kabala*
G A B R I E L L E (Girl)   G A B R I E L L E
3 1 2 2 1 5 3 3 5   3 1 2 20 10 5 12 12 5
= 25 = 7   = 70 = 7

The same number comes out with both systems and the descriptions will be: for Unit system, 7, positive number of Moon, Chapter 4, page 53; for Kabala, Chapter 4, page 44, influence of the sign Sagittarius.

Unit System   *Kabala*
G A B R I E L (Boy)   G A B R I E L
3 1 2 2 1 5 3   3 1 2 20 10 5 12
= 17 = 8   = 53 = 8

Both numbers are again the same. The 8 in the Unit system will respond to the influence of Saturn, Chapter 4, page 50; the 8 in the Kabala vibrates to the sign Capricorn, Chapter 4, page 45.

Unit System   *Kabala*
M A U D E   M A U D E
4 1 6 4 5   13 1 6 4 5
= 20 = 2   = 29 = 11

With the Unit system the number 2 shows the Moon negative vibration, Chapter 4, page 53;

NAMES AND NUMBERS 35

whilst the Kabala shows the number 11 under the influence of Neptune, Chapter 4, page 47.

Unit System	*Kabala*
M A U D	M A U D
4 1 6 4	13 1 6 4
= 15 = 6	= 24 = 6

The same number results from each system. The number 6 in each system is the same, it brings in the influence of the planet Venus, Chapter 4, page 44.

Unit System	*Kabala*
P A U L E T T E	P A U L E T T E
8 1 6 3 5 4 4 5	17 1 6 12 5 22 22 5
= 36 = 9	= 90 = 9

In the Unit system the number 9 brings in the influence of Aquarius, Chapter 4, page 46; also the Kabala shows the number 9, under the influence of the sign Aquarius, Chapter 4, page 46.

Unit System	*Kabala*
P A U L I N E	P A U L I N E
8 1 6 3 1 5 5	17 1 6 12 10 14 5
= 29 = 11 = 2	= 65 = 11

The number 2 in the Unit system responds to the influence of the Moon negative, Chapter 4, page 53; the number 11 in the Kabala shows the influence of the planet Neptune, Chapter 4, page 47.

Unit System	*Kabala*
D O R O T H Y	D O R O T H Y
4 7 2 7 4 8 1	4 16 20 16 22 8 10
= 33 = 6	= 96 = 15

The number 6 in the Unit system gives the influence of the planet Venus, Chapter 4, page 44; whilst the number 15 in the Kabala gives the influence of the planet Saturn, Chapter 4, page 50.

Unit System	*Kabala*
L I L Y	L I L Y
3 1 3 1	12 10 12 10
= 8	= 44 = 8

Both numbers the same, 8 in the Unit system shows the planet Saturn, Chapter 4, page 50; 8 in the Kabala shows the sign Capricorn, Chapter 4, page 45.

Unit System	*Kabala*
A D A	A D A
1 4 1	1 4 1
= 6	= 6

Both numbers are again the same. The 6 in the Unit system and in the Kabala both respond to the influence of the planet Venus, Chapter 4, page 44.

Unit System	*Kabala*
A L I C E	A L I C E
1 3 1 2 5	1 12 10 11 5
= 12 = 3	= 39 = 12

In the Unit system the number 3 responds to the influence of the planet Jupiter, Chapter 4, page 43. In the Kabala the number 12 responds to the vibration of the sign Pisces, Chapter 4, page 48.

Unit System   *Kabala*
D A I S Y   D A I S Y
4 1 1 3 1   4 1 10 21 10
= 10 = 1   = 46 = 10

The number 1 in the Unit system shows the influence of the Sun positive, Chapter 4, page 54; whilst the number 10 in the Kabala shows the vibration of the planet Uranus, Chapter 4, page 47.

Unit System   *Kabala*
E L I Z A B E T H   E L I Z A B E T H
5 3 1 7 1 2 5 4 8   5 12 10 7 1 2 5 22 8
= 36 = 9   = 72 = 9

The number is the same with each system. In the Unit system 9 responds to the planet Mars, Chapter 4, page 51; whilst in the Kabala it shows forth the influence of the sign Aquarius, Chapter 4, page 46.

Sufficient name illustrations have now been given to demonstrate the principles involved and to show the reader how to interpret the Christian or Forename in terms of Character. If there is more than one Christian or Forename, then THAT NAME WHICH IS USED in preference to the others will be the main significator of the character; the other names will show subsidiary influences which will not be anywhere near as powerful.

There is, however, an ancillary factor which has to be taken into account and that is when a Christian or Forename is shortened or an alternative or nick-name given, WHICH IS CONSTANTLY IN USE. There will be no lessening of the primary influence of the main Christian or Forename, but an addition of the influence of shortened name or nick-name, thus:—

Unit System		Kabala
T E D	(for Edward)	T E D
4 5 4		22 5 4
= 13 = 4		= 31 = 4

Both come to the same number. 4 in the Unit system is the influence of the Sun, negative, Chapter 4, page 54; and 4 in the Kabala is the sign Scorpio, Chapter 4, page 43.

In this case the number is the same as for the full name of Edward (see page 32) and hence there is an accentuation of the planetary or sign influence.

Unit System		Kabala
R O B E R T	(Full Name)	R O B E R T
2 7 2 5 2 4		20 16 2 5 20 22
= 22 = 4		= 85 = 13
B O B	(Shortened)	B O B
2 7 2		2 16 2
= 11 = 2		= 20

The shortened name of BOB brings in two different numbers from the full name of ROBERT. In the Unit system the number 2 will exercise power and bring in the influence of the sign Virgo; whilst in the Kabala the number 20 will operate and bring in the influence of the Moon. These descriptions are given in Chapter 4, pages 41 and 53 respectively.

Unit System   *Kabala*
B E T T Y   (for Elizabeth)   B E T   T   Y
2 5 4 4 1   2 5 22 22 10
= 16 = 7   = 61 = 7

The number is the same for either system. In the Unit system it will show the influence of the Moon positive, Chapter 4, page 53, and in the Kabala the influence of the sign Sagittarius, Chapter 4, page 44.

In the case of the full name Elizabeth the number came to 9 (see page 37) and hence by using Betty, an added influence is brought into play.

Sufficient examples have been given here to enable you to work out the numerical value of any name by reference to the tables in Chapter 2.

CHAPTER FOUR

NUMBERS AND CHARACTER

In-so-far as an individual is concerned, the effect that a specific number has upon his or her life can be demonstrated in terms of character, of health, of personal associations such as marriage, relatives, friends and enemies, of money, whether it be earned through work or business, or gained by speculation, investment, gift or legacy, of work or vocation itself, of travel, and of mental or artistic ability.

The zodiacal or planetary influence of each number from 1 to 22 will give a specific vibration and, in terms of character, these will be as shown in the following descriptions which have been written as applying to YOU to be the more easily explainable and understandable.

The preceding chapter explained how to find your own specific number from your name; thus you will be able to apply the specific character vibration of that number to yourself. In the same way you will be able to learn the characters of others.

The number ONE (planetary influence Mercury, ☿) rules the brain and the mind and hence will give good intellectual capacity. It will attract to pursuits and work of a mental rather than of a physical character and is associated with learning, education and the teaching or training of others, and gives capacity for the holding of executive and administrative positions. There is a combination of independence and yet of adaptability, a capacity to acquire a myriad of facts and yet be able to coagulate these into one fixed line of action should the latter be desired. Knowledge will be gained through observation and travel and considerable travel is denoted although much of this will be of a short or medium long distance nature rather than of a long distance or overseas character. There will be a capacity for writing and certain forms of literary work, for journalism and contact with newspapers and associated publications.

The number Two (zodiacal influence the sign Virgo,♍) gives you a natural power of discrimination and perception which will express itself in a natural manner through business and associated channels. You will be able to carry out the details of affairs without losing sight of the ultimate goal towards which you are working. You can carry out any routine set you by others and, when necessary, can evolve a routine of your own proving satisfactory to all concerned. It does not take you long to weigh up the pros and cons of affairs and your power of perception enables you to see beneath the surface to the truth that others may try to hide. You are appreciative of neatness and tidiness and prefer proper discipline to lackadaisical methods. The sign will cause you to be critical and you will need to use discretion in the expressing of criticism, for anything of a hurtful nature, even though it may be true, could be taken exception to by the ones concerned, and misunderstandings could arise.

The number THREE (zodiacal influence, the sign Libra, ♎) gives you a strong desire for peace and harmony and causes you to be sensitive to anything of a deliberately discordant nature. You are naturally courteous and desirous of being on good terms with other people, but you will always need to maintain a proper spirit of independence so as to prevent certain people from imposing upon you who are aware of your natural disinclination to enter into arguments or disputes. A tendency towards giving way to the line of least resistance will need to be faced up to and overcome. You will be attracted towards the social and public sides of life and should do all you can to further these interests. Do not let domestic matters or the attempted domination of those in your surroundings have a restrictive influence over you. You can be very adaptable but you can also be very easily upset by adverse criticism or temporary rebuffs, and inclined to take things more to heart than you should do.

The number FOUR (zodiacal influence, the sign Scorpio ♏) gives you a degree of reserve and in certain respects will cause you to be secretive, although this will not necessarily interfere with your everyday associations. It shows that you will display considerable resourcefulness in the handling of people and affairs and as a result will work through difficulties somewhat more easily than may be anticipated, either by yourself or others.

You will express more resistance and fighting capacity than those around you may recognise, and should anyone attempt to take an unfair advantage of you they will be extremely surprised at the resistance you will put forth in the protecting of your own interests. You have the courage of your own convictions to say and do the things you consider to be correct, will always try to push ahead with affairs in your own way and will not let others impose upon you or force you to do things against your own desires.

The number FIVE (planetary influence, Jupiter, ♃) will give you a broad and tolerant view upon life and will strengthen your spirit of comradeship. You will always be willing to help others in trouble but will need to maintain commonsense as there will be times when certain persons will seek to take an unfair advantage of your goodness of spirit. Religious and philosophical matters will appeal to you, there will be a strong desire for travel and it is possible for the missionary spirit to be strong. The spirit of optimism will invariably be marked but on occasions can cause you to experience loss when you permit yourself to take certain possibilities too much for granted or rely too much upon the element of luck or chance. The main essential to bear in mind isthat whilst keeping optimistic you should also be practical.

The number SIX (planetary influence, Venus ♀) being ruled by the planet of affection, of love and of beauty, will cause your desire for companionship to be exceedingly strong and, therefore, all matters to do with the affections, with marriage and with friendships will prove to be very importand and a great deal of your happiness or unhappiness in life will depend upon the nature of the ties and associations which you form. If these are of a constructive and helpful nature they will bring happiness and enable you to make considerable progress in life, but should they be of an impulsive and unwise character, then they will bring unhappiness, depression and an interference with your progress. There will be an appreciation of the artistic side of affairs even if circumstances prevent you from developing any form of art yourself. Sometimes the artistic faculty will find scope in painting, decoration, etc., even in the preparing of foods in a manner both appetising and appealing to the sight as well as to the taste.

The number SEVEN (zodiacal influence, the sign Sagittarius ♐) causes you to be frank and outspoken with a very strong desire for liberty and freedom of thought and action, as well as for the maintaining of personal independence. Under normal circumstances you will usually adhere to the ordinary customs and conventions of life, but should affairs become too monotonous, or should there be any degree of what appears to you to be unfair restriction or limitation, a spirit of rebellion will occur and you will then say and do things and bring about changes without letting the immediate results affect you too strongly.

You are naturally active, energetic and optimistic but you will need to control impulsive and hasty inclinations whilst you should not give way unduly to restlessness. You are naturally self-reliant and you can inspire others by the example you set. An interest in sport is denoted.

The number EIGHT (zodiacal influence, the sign Capricorn ♑) causes you to be ambitious, practical and in some ways acquisitive. There will be a more or less natural gravitation towards the holding of positions of authority and trust, but you should not permit others to shift unfair burdens of responsibility onto your shoulders and then take the credit and benefits for themselves. It is a sign showing that you can work hard and long and will invariably set an example to others that they will find it exceptionally difficult to emulate.

For this reason you will also experience difficulties when you want others to carry out work for you, as they will never do things in quite the same way as yourself or take quite the same pains you do, nor will they exhibit a like degree of thoroughness.

Sometimes you will know what it is to feel depressed and unhappy, and will temporarily lose heart and wonder if there is anything in life worth working for. During these periods do not shun the company of others but take part in social affairs.

The number NINE (zodiacal influence, the sign Aquarius ♒) shows that you are thoughtful, reflective and studious. Many of your thoughts and ideas will be in advance of those of your companions and yet will not interfere with your friendships and associations, in fact you will find that those with whom you associate will often look to you for advice regarding their problems and you may need to use a degree of firmness to prevent imposition. Discretion will be required regarding the taking on of obligations and liabilities, expecially of a financial character, where friends and relatives are concerned.

From a general standpoint the sign causes you to be cheerful, sincere and optimistic, but in a quiet, rather than an ostentatious manner. You have some very strong likes and dislikes, and will be very firm where your principles, convictions and lines of action are concerned, and will put up a deal of resistance when others try to force you to do things or to agree to conditions that are against your own inclinations.

The number TEN (planetary influence, Uranus ♅) shows that somehat erratic tendencies are denoted. Whilst there will be an undoubted brilliance of thought and inspiration, a capacity for making quick and constructive decisions in an emergency, and for carrying these decisions into action without loss of time, under ordinary circumstances when nothing of very great importance is manifesting, there will be a difficulty in exercising adaptability to such conditions and hence there will be a making of impulsive and unwise decisions regarding changes and in connection with prevailing associations. As a result sudden upsets and disputes will occur, there will be a disturbing of working or business interests and a danger of a loss of job or position, whilst personal ties and associations can be strained, sometimes to actual breaking point. In many respects you will be a "law unto yourself" and will go your own way irrespective of the desires or commands of others; in fact any attempt on the part of people to force you to follow their way will only make you go in the opposite direction.

The number ELEVEN (planetary influence, Neptune ψ) will intensify your insight into affairs and enable you to gauge the outcome of a given line of action in an almost uncanny manner. It shows that you will be able, sometimes without hardly being aware of it, to influence other people by your mental and oral suggestions and in so doing will get them to react and do things that are in accord with your own desires. Discretion will, however, be required in the using of this power of suggestion, for otherwise, should you be tempted to influence other people to do things to suit a selfish end you could bring a tantalising and unpleasant future reaction. You will have much latent psychic ability, which you can express as a result of proper development, for the planet gives a capacity for clairvoyance, sometimes for trance mediumship, and also for psychometry.

The number TWELVE (zodiacal influence, the sign Pisces ♓) shows that you are idealistic and peaceably inclined. You can, however, be rather sensitive and there will be extremes of temperament and ability. Sometimes you will be extremely cheerful and optimistic and when you express this side of your nature, together with a degree of sympathy and understanding for others who are in trouble or difficulty, you will create considerable popularity and will make a great deal of progress.

On the other hand you can give way to extreme sensitiveness and allow yourself to feel hurt at the careless or thoughtless speech or actions of others and will try to cover this up by expressing an apparent air of indifference which will be rather puzzling to those around you, who will not be aware of having done anything to warrant being ignored. When you permit anything of this nature you will lose some of your popularity and certain of your friends, and misunderstandings will occur in a way you do not at all desire.

The number THIRTEEN (zodiacal influence, the sign Aries ♈) causes you to be independent, self-willed, active and desirous of being in command of affairs. You are courageous by nature and not likely to be afraid of facing danger when it arises, but you should not create conditions that bring it or that would lead to disturbing and unpleasant consequences. The combining of intellectual with physical activity will enable you to effect progress and to bring altered conditions in accord with your own desires. You can set an example to others that they will be pleased to follow when you combine tact with enthusiasm. If, however, you let aggressive inclinations, undue independence, or impulse, decide your line of action you can create unfriendliness, can lose support and hence interfere with your normal progress.

You will always want to fight against conditions of an unfair and restrictive nature.

The number FOURTEEN (zodiacal influence, the sign Taurus, ♉) causes you to be practical, industrious, and in many ways capable of exercising considerable patience where the more important interests of life are concerned. You have ability to plan out affairs ahead and to allow proper time for the maturing of your plans. You can also bring about a perfecting of the details relating to material and financial matters. Quite a number of your desires and wishes will be associated with money. You possess the courage of your own convictions and opposition from others will only tend to fix them more firmly in your mind. At the same time it would be wrong to term your disposition an unreasonable one, as you are prepared to consider the suggestions of others on their own merits, and if they appeal to you, adopt them. You will do so however, as and when you see fit.

The number FIFTEEN (planetary influence, Saturn ♄) in its influence over your character shows that you are serious, reflective, somewhat introspective and yet have the inner capacity to hold positions of responsibility and authority and to carry out duties efficiently. Life will not always be easy for you. You will have to fight against restrictions, limitations and delays, but by the exercising of patience you will find yourself overcoming the varying difficulties that confront you, and as a result of persistence will bring about progress. Saturn rules the latter part of life and distinctly shows that this part of life will bring the rewards or disappointments of the efforts, or lack of effort, during the first half of life. It is a planet that attracts towards political and kindred affairs and gives very great organising ability. It invariably denotes that a very advanced age will be reached and that time will be on your side in the making of plans and in the putting forth of effort, therefore you can afford to be painstaking and will always be able to take the long rather than the short view of affairs.

The number SIXTEEN (planetary influence, Mars ♂) mainly signifies so far as your character is concerned, that you have courage. This will be of both a physical and a mental nature and no matter what the odds may be you will always face them and do your best to overcome your adversary, whether it be circumstances or a person. Nevertheless, it will not be easy to restrain impulse or to tone down quickness of temper and as a result of giving way to these you will experience many upsets and changes, and your emotional and home life will not always be happy. You are suited for adventure, for exploration, for taking part in anything that is active and that keeps you on the move. When circumstances temporarily thrust you into a kind of quiet backwater you will rebel, sometimes violently and, figuratively speaking, will either do the disappearing trick yourself or be thrown out by others who resent their peace and quietness being disturbed.

The number SEVENTEEN (zodiacal influence, the sign Gemini ♊) indicates that you are active both physically and mentally. You will have a strong desire for variety and change but it will be unwise to allow this desire to get out of hand. An effort should always be made to maintain continuity of thought and action, and you should not alter objectives unless there is some very real and weighty reason for so doing. Otherwise you will find that you can interfere with the progress of affairs, can put forth a lot of effort and get very little in return. You should regulate the number of subjects you take up, for if you have too many things on hand at one time certain of them must perforce be neglected, particularly when circumstances compel attention upon those of greater importance. Hence valuable time, thought and effort will be sacrificed which has been devoted to those interests being given up.

The number EIGHTEEN (zodiacal influence, the sign Cancer ♋) signifies that there is a strong degree of emotion in your nature. You have a very vivid imagination and will be able to recall clearly and easily many of the events and conditions which have occurred in the past but should not allow yourself to dwell too much upon the past. You should utilize the knowledge gained from past experiences, to deal with and to regulate present affairs, and to plan out future activities. Matters to do with the home and family side of life will always be of great importance and will influence many of your decisions and actions, whilst there will be a great appreciation of domestic comfort and harmony. You can also do many things yourself towards creating domestic comfort and making others feel at home when they are in your surroundings. The sign gives you a very good memory, much tenacity of thought and purpose and enables you to use your imagination so as to create publicity either for yourself or for others.

The number NINETEEN (zodiacal influence, the sign Leo ♌) gives you a great deal of natural ambition causing you to be desirous of making good headway and progress in life. There will always be a more or less automatic gravitation towards the occupying of a central position according to your sphere of life, whilst you will always do the best that you can, no matter what circumstances of life arise, and will invariably try to appear at your best when you are with others. You have a natural degree of pride and dignity and can express the principle of loyalty towards others and towards any cause you may espouse. There will, however, be times when you will need to control hasty and passionate impulses and inclinations, for should these be given way to, setbacks and downfalls can occur. Nevertheless, once you realise you have made a mistake or error of judgment you can take quick steps to bring about a retrieving of the situation. Your power of organisation is good and will help you in the handling of business and private affairs.

The number TWENTY (planetary influence, the Moon ☽) in its rule over your character shows that there will be alternate periods of activity, enthusiasm and expression with others when you will feel you want to do nothing, when you will lack incentive and when there will seem to be no inspiration. This ebb and flow of feeling and action is quite in sympathy with the phases of the Moon, which show an upsurge of power and strength as it goes from the New to the Full and then a decrease of energy until apparent stagnation occurs as the Moon goes through the waning period from Full to New. Home, family and domestic interests will take a deal of your thought and attention, whilst this lunar influence is favourable for matters to do with the land, agriculture, dairy farming, etc. You will have a natural sympathy for others, and also for animals, especially when they are suffering, for what may be called the "mothering spirit" will always be strong.

The number TWENTY-ONE (planetary influence, the Sun ☉) in its influence over the character draws out the sense of power and hence you will always have the desire to exercise authority and a degree of domination over others, and during the course of your life's development you will do so. Nevertheless, when you are in a position of authority you will need to see that you use this in a constructive and proper manner, resisting any inclination to be autocratic or domineering. If the latter is given way to, not only will you make enemies, but you will interfere with the finer rewards which life can give you. You will be attracted to and have an interest in children and in education, art, theatrical and associated interests and be able to do quite a deal of good if you live up to the higher dictates of your nature. The principle of leadership will be marked and if used constructively will bring recognition and possibly fame.

The number TWENTY-TWO (planetary influence, the Earth ⊕) shows that the season of the year when you were born will have a determining influence over your character. If born in the Spring you will have initiative, and the spirit of enterprise will be marked throughout the course of your life, but you will find yourself having to learn many lessons in your handling of affairs and in your association with other people before you acquire perception and discrimination.

If born in the Summer you will have organising ability and the capacity to hold positions of authority. You will have a degree of pride and dignity and it will be relatively easy to obtain recognition of your abilities and the years from 40 to 60 will bring you to the zenith of your power.

If born in the Autumn you will have quite a deal of natural knowledge and understanding, the factors of comparison, discrimination and arbitration will be the key-notes of your life, but you will need to set determinative aims if you are to make real progress and you will want a degree of companionship.

If born in the Winter you will have the wisdom of the ages. Many times you will be lonely because others will not reach up to your standard of thought and comprehension. The first half of life will be hard, but the second half can bring a realising of earlier ambitions and desires.

CHAPTER FIVE

YOUR LOVE AND MARRIAGE NUMBER

In all the interests of life those to do with love and marriage are by far the most important, ranking equal to health on the one hand and to money on the other. The desire for companionship and affection is invariably exceedingly strong in the human make-up and much of the happiness or unhappiness in life will spring from the making of either a satisfactory attachment, leading to a successful marriage, or to the forming of an unwise association leading to emotional upsets and a possible frustration of marriage or to the bringing about of an unsuitable marriage with subsequent divorce.

When we know our own love and marriage number we become aware of our own prospects and this knowledge, if used correctly, can aid us in mitigating or even offsetting the unfavourable possibilities and of assisting those of a constructive and helpful nature.

By knowing the love and marriage number and its attributes of the prospective or actual partner, we are enabled in the former instance to see whether the mutual vibrations are helpful or the reverse and if necessary to make a decision; whilst in the latter instance, by knowing the potentialities of the marriage partner's love and marriage number, we are enabled, if we so choose, to act so that there is a mitigating of adverse significations, thus helping in the creating of greater harmony and hence of greater love and compassion, or, if the combination is harmonious, to bring about a realising of mutual desires and wishes where children, social and public interests, and other matters of importance are concerned.

To know our love and marriage number it is necessary to take ALL our Christian or Forenames and to obtain the totals of the numbers from both the systems, the Unit system and the Kabala—the former system being used to find the harmonies and antipathies between numbers, and the latter system giving the description of love and marital possibilities according to the planetary or zodiacal influence that corresponds to the number.

Of course, if one only has one Christian or Forename then the ultimate number derived from the addition of all the numbers of the letters of that name, as shows in chapter Three, will apply. Thus, in the case of the name EDWARD (see page 32), the total of which is 4 in each system, the 4 of the Unit system applied to the Table showing harmonies, antipathies, etc., on page 60, signifies that 4 vibrates to and harmonises with 6, attracts those whose number is 1 or 8, disagrees with or is antipathetic to those whose number is 3 or 5, and is passive to the charms, virtues or vices of those whose number is 2, 7 or 9.

When there are two or more Christian or Forenames, then each name must be taken separately, and the total of each added together so as to obtain a second Unit and Kabala total. This is performed as follows:

Unit System

```
E D W A R D      W I L L I A M
5 4 6 1 2 4      6 1 3 3 1 1 4
  = 22 = 4         = 19 = 10 = 1
           4 + 1 = 5
```

The number 5 therefore becomes the love and marriage number, and the numbers that harmonise, disagree with it, or are neutral, are found in the Table of Harmonies and Antipathies, page 60.

Kabala

```
E D W A R  D      W I  L  L  I  A  M
5 4 6 1 20 4      6 10 12 12 10 1 13
  = 40 = 4          = 64 = 10
           4 + 10 = 14
```

The number 14 being the number shown according to the Kabala, the indications regarding love and marriage are influenced by the sign Taurus.

The attributes of each number under the Kabala system are given later in this chapter.

A few more examples will be given so that the reader may become familiar with the process.

Unit System

```
R  O  B  E  R  T           H  E  N  R  Y
2  7  2  5  2  4           8  5  5  2  1
   = 22 = 4                   = 21 = 3
              4 + 3 = 7
```

See harmonies, etc., in Table on page 60.

Kabala

```
R   O  B  E  R   T          H  E  N   R   Y
20  16 2  5  20  22         8  5  14  20  10
    = 85 = 13                   = 57 = 12
              13 + 12 = 25 = 7
```

As the sum of the two name totals comes to over 22, *i.e.* to 25, it must be further reduced by the addition of the units so as to bring it to 22 or under. In this instance it reduces to 7 and this will be the love and marriage number according to the Kabala.

Unit System

```
A  L  I  C  E              J  E  A  N  N  E
1  3  1  2  5              1  5  1  5  5  5
   = 12 = 3                    = 22 = 4
              3 + 4 = 7
```

See harmonies, etc., in Table on page 60

Kabala

```
A  L   I   C   E           J   E  A  N   N   E
1  12  10  11  5           10  5  1  14  14  5
    = 39 = 12                    = 49 = 13
              12 + 13 = 25 = 7
```

The same process is repeated with these totals as with the previous name and hence the vibration will be the same, love and marriage being under the influence of the sign Sagittarius.

Unit System

```
M A R G A R E T        R O S E
4 1 2 3 1 2 5 4        2 7 3 5
   = 22 = 4              = 17 = 8
       4 + 8 = 12 = 3
```

See harmonies, etc., in Table below.

Kabala

```
M  A  R  G A  R  E  T       R  O  S  E
13 1 20 3 1 20 5 22         20 16 21 5
     = 85 = 13                 = 62 = 8
       13 + 8 = 21
```

When there are more than two Christian or Forenames the same principle is followed but the total of each name is added and the final result from both the Unit and the Kabala systems used.

TABLE OF NUMBER HARMONIES AND ANTIPATHIES UNDER THE UNIT SYSTEM

1 vibrates to 9; attracts 4 and 8; and disagrees with 6 and 7. It is passive to 2, 3 and 5.

2 vibrates to 8; attracts 7 and 9; and disagrees with 5. It is passive to 1, 3, 4 and 6.

3 vibrates to 7; attracts 5, 6 and 9; and disagrees with 4 and 8. It is passive to 1 and 2.

4 vibrates to 6; attracts 1 and 8; and disagrees with 3 and 5. It is passive to 2, 7 and 9.

5 vibrates to another 5; attracts 3 and 9; and disagrees with 2 and 4. It is passive to 1, 6, 7 and 8.

6 vibrates to 4; attracts 3 and 9; and disagrees with 1 and 8. It is passive to 2, 5 and 7.

7 vibrates to 3; attracts 2 and 6; and disagrees with 1 and 9. It is passive to 4, 5 and 8.

8 vibrates to 2; attracts 1 and 4; and disagrees with 3 and 6. It is passive to 5, 7 and 9.

9 vibrates to 1; attracts 2, 3 and 6; and disagrees with 7. It is passive to 4, 5 and 8.

YOUR LOVE AND MARRIAGE NUMBER

Explaining the above:

(*a*) A number that vibrates to another shows that there is considerable mutual attraction and the marriage will be very favourable.

(*b*) A number that attracts another shows that the two people are well suited to each other.

(*c*) A number that disagrees with another shows that the union will call for a great deal of diplomacy, if it is to be attended with any measure of success.

(*d*) Where a number is passive, it merely means that numerology offers no opinion, there being no outstanding influence for good or bad.

(*e*) Of course, if the two numbers are alike, it is a foregone conclusion that the union will be very favourable.

The following attributes of the Love and Marriage number are based upon the planetary and zodiacal influences associated with each number.

The number ONE shows that the desire for variety in love affairs will be marked and hence it will not be too easy to bring about a lasting attachment which will be productive of marriage. You will be attracted towards intellectual types and yet, because of the intellectual bias, there can be an absence of passional warmth which, despite your own intellectual conception of affairs, you will desire. Hence it will be somewhat difficult to bring about desired developments. The marriage partner can be contacted whilst on a journey or as a result of attending a lecture or discussion group. Sometimes under the Mercury vibration the partner is a cousin. Once marriage has been brought about there will be need for exercising a degree of forethought and discrimination in order to ensure that the marriage shall last for, with an absence of passional warmth, misunderstandings could lead to a degree of bitterness and even to separation.

The number Two shows that you will use quite a deal of discrimination in matters to do with the affectional and marital sides of life. There will be an attraction towards marriage and a desire for certain of the amenities and comforts normally associated with the marital side of life. Affectional and marital disturbances can, however, occur as a result either of the criticism of the prospective or actual partner or because of criticism or interference of others who play some part in your normal everyday life. If these conditions become too pronounced, then unhappiness will be experienced; but if you exercise a combination of firmness with sympathy, then troubles and difficulties can be overcome. The best type of partner is shown to be someone who is intellectual but who can also give thought to what may be termed "creature comforts" and who will be practical so far as financial and kindred matters are concerned.

The number Three shows that your desire for companionship and affection is strong and hence showing that there will be a natural attraction towards the marital side of life. You will entertain somewhat idealistic views regarding marriage, but should always maintain a degree of practicality as otherwise there can be either a difficulty in bringing about developments or in maintaining ties once they are formed. It is a sign as well that will seem to give a peculiar attraction towards certain types of person, of the opposite sex, and hence it will again be necessary to see that this sense of fascination does not cause you to form attachments again interfering with prevailing ties or causing complications not altogether anticipated or desired. On the other hand, if you let your knowledge of human nature guide you, you can make a good choice of partner and will find that that partner will aid you regarding any interests of a social, public or kindred nature in which you may take part.

The number FOUR shows that the affectional and emotional desires are very strong and hence will attract you towards marriage, but you will need to use some discretion in your making of attachments and in your choice of marriage partner as you will find that difficulties will be encountered through the jealousy and antagonism of certain individuals and it will not be too easy to bring about desired developments. Personal impulses will require regulating and you should not always take the advances of others too literally nor link them up with the possibility of marriage. The correct type of partner is shown to be of an active temperament with quite a deal of physical courage, interested quite possibly in occult affairs and conceivably with certain mechanical interests as well. Resourcefulness will be a marked characteristic but they can be somewhat possessive and jealous, and because of this, emotional upsets and unpleasantness can occur.

The number FIVE shows that love affairs and marriage will be productive of quite a degree of happiness and of benefit. There will be a strong desire for affection, but the factor of sincerity will count for a lot and despite a natural desire for companionship previous to marriage, the commonsense view of affairs will keep this desire within bounds and thus give a better opportunity for a constructive association to develop to the point of engagement and later of marriage. In some respects interests of a philosophical and religious nature will play their part and the marriage partner can be met whilst attending church or a religious ceremony or through activities connected with the religious side of affairs. Marriage is shown to be very helpful. There will be love and sympathy from the marriage partner and benefit through the help of the partner in connection with vocational and financial matters.

The number SIX shows that companionship being the keynote of this number's influence, there will be a natural attraction towards certain members of the opposite sex and the desire for love and affection will be very strong. There will, however, be a need to control sudden impulses for, otherwise, attachments of an unsatisfactory nature will be formed and, should these be allowed to bring about marriage, the outcome would not be as happy or successful as anticipated. Yet if the difference between fascination and true love can be distinguished, real happiness, both before and after marriage, is signified. This number, however, is essentially a weak number and shows that emotional and sexual temptations will occur and if circumstances bring a compulsory period or periods of separation from the marriage partner after marriage, the desire for companionship can cause the forming of temporary associations which, if permitted to go too far, could lead to a disturbing of the marriage tie.

The number SEVEN signifies that there will be more than one affectional attachment or love affair and it sometimes shows the consummation of more than one marriage. It indicates that interests to do with sport, outdoor life, animals and birds, travel and to some extent religion can be the means of meeting the prospective and actual partner. Although in its general influence the sign exercises a favourable vibration it does show that before the real partner is contacted and marriage consummated, there will be a making and breaking of associations and it is possible for one of these breaks to be caused by the prospective partner going away, either through travel or in connection with vocation, and failing to make a renewal of the contact. One thing is shown to be of great importance, and that is that after marriage any difference of race or religion should not be permitted to cause misunderstanding.

The number EIGHT shows that certain of your ambitions are associated with the affectional and marital side of affairs and that as a result of marriage you will aim to bring about a developing of business, social and public affairs with the co-operation of the partner. At the same time it may not be too easy to find the right type of partner and hence delays and obstructive conditions can arise, both in the actual forming of attachments and as regards the consummation of marriage. It is possible for the marriage partner to be older than yourself and for marriage to take place somewhat later in life than is usually considered to be the average age for marriage. You will need to give some thought to the health of the partner and should so regulate domestic and kindred matters that some of the pressure of everyday affairs is taken away. You will also find that at times the partner will not be too demonstrative from the affectional standpoint but this will not detract from their sincerity of affection.

The number NINE in its rule over love affairs and marriage shows that many of your hopes and wishes will be associated with these interests of life and you will want to bring about a developing of associations so that marriage can be consummated. As a result of marriage you will also find it easier to bring about a realising of other hopes and wishes to do with the social and public sides of life and with finance and business, as the help of the marriage partner will prove to be invaluable in these respects. Yet difficulties will be encountered in first of all making an attachment that can be developed up to the requisite end of marriage. In early life the sign shows an attraction to persons of the opposite sex who are older than yourself and some discrimination will be required to see that the disparity in age is not too pronounced, as this could bring future unhappiness. If marriage is not consummated reasonably early in life then, as age advances you will find that the attraction will veer round to those of the opposite sex who are younger, but a degree of prejudice can occur from others associated with the desired partner.

The number TEN being the number of romance shows that there will be quite a number of love affairs in the life and some of these can be of quite a hectic and outstanding nature, but as the number also causes sudden upsets and breaks, the pathway of love will not run too smoothly and hence several affairs are signified before marriage is finally brought about. When it does take place it is likely to be in a sudden and unexpected manner and even after it has been achieved there will be a danger of sudden upsets. If these are permitted to go to an extreme, separation or even divorce can occur. Therefore, you will need to be watchful as it will be so easy for things to go awry. particularly as, owing to the romantic tendency in your nature, you can be attracted to two or even more persons of the opposite sex at the same time.

The number ELEVEN in its influence over love affairs and the condition of marriage, will be somewhat peculiar. It tends to bring about a forming of platonic associations, both before and after marriage, or circumstances can seem to compel a degree of secrecy. You will also find that your own power of mental and oral suggestion will have an influence over those towards whom you are attracted and hence, unless you are morally strong, can cause you to be tempted to do things to gain a selfish end. In giving way to such temptations, however, future trouble and unrest can be built up. Alternatively, there will be occasions when you yourself will be receptive to the suggestions of others and hence can experience some form of deception from the one to whom you are attracted or even married. The outcome of marital affairs will depend very greatly upon the trend of financial and business interests. If these go awry then the marriage can suffer.

The number TWELVE gives an idealistic conception of affectional and marital conditions and shows that you have the capacity to make many sacrifices in order to bring about a developing of affectional issues; it signifies that you will experience many vicissitudes and the trend of affectional matters will not run as smoothly or happily as you desire, and your spirit of sacrifice can in certain instances be abused in a very unfair manner by those to whom you give love and affection. There is a strong indication of more than one affectional attachment, but breaks can occur either through the unwise or even selfish actions of the prospective or actual partner, or because of your disagreement with the partner's mode of life or activities and a sudden realising that temperamental differences would only be productive of unhappiness. You need a partner who will be able to blend practicality with a degree of ambition and yet who will give some thought to domestic and private affairs, but the danger is that those whom you contact will not seem to have the necessary incentive to bring about progress desired, or, if they have, they will be already married or tied in some way.

The number THIRTEEN shows that you are somewhat idealistic regarding matters to do with the affections and marriage, but may not always be practical. Certain types of the opposite sex will seem to have a rather peculiar attraction or fascination for you and if you do not exercise proper control you can give way to inclinations to form attachments interfering with existing ties. A degree of emotional impulse is strongly shown and is intensified by your natural desire for companionship. Affectional and marital interests will not always run too smoothly as the prospective or actual partner will usually be active and energetic and on occasions this activity will conflict with your own desire to pursue affairs in a reasonably quiet and unhurried manner. Any attempt at domination on the side of the partner will be productive of friction and temperamental upsets.

The number FOURTEEN will enhance the desire for affection, but also gives a sense of discrimination and hence attachments will not be too lightly entered into. It is not a flirtatious number, but shows an appreciation of sincerity and can give sincerity in return, therefore once an association is made there will be an intent to make it permanent and, if possible, to bring about marriage. Should a break occur, either through circumstances or because the prospective partner lacks the same sincerity as yourself, you will suffer rather severely and it will take quite a considerable time to overcome the sense of hurt and to take steps towards the forming of another attachment. Usually, with marriage, it will be a marriage for life and if the marriage has developed from a love match, as is quite possible, then there is not likely to be a desire for a second marriage should the marriage partner die first.

The number FIFTEEN will exercise a retarding and delaying influence. In love affairs there will be a difficulty in making a requisite approach to someone of the opposite sex, and though the desire and the liking may be strong it will not be easy to express the desire in words or action and hence opportunities for the forming of attachments can be lost, particularly in early life. As age advances it will be easier to make the approach as a result of past experience and a satisfactory attachment and marriage can be brought about, the latter being of a lasting nature. You are not likely to experience passionate flirtations and love affairs, for despite an inner ardency you will not be likely to attract those who would respond, but on the other hand you can bring about a marriage with a partner who will be constant and who will be more likely to stick to you through times of difficulty.

The number SIXTEEN invariably gives an ardency of affection and, therefore, more than one love affair or attachment is signified. There will be a tendency to rush into associations and sometimes to mistake fascination for love. On occasions an inclination to flirt, just for the fun of the thing, will be very strong, and so long as this does not go beyond certain limits no harm will result, but should the passional side of the nature be allowed to become too marked, future complications could occur. Once a definite attachment has been formed and engagement brought about you should not let temporary inclinations of an amorous nature intervene as to permit this would be to bring about a possible upsetting of the association and engagement. The same remarks will apply, and in an even stronger manner, after marriage, which, from a general standpoint, is shown to take place early in life.

The number SEVENTEEN shows that more than one affectional attachment will occur and there is a strong indication of more than one marriage. You will, however, need to exercise discretion in the making of attachments as, owing to your desire for change and variety, you can permit sudden fascinations to influence you and hence can make attachments which, after a time, pall and are creative of complications which will not be too easily overcome, especially should you wish to effect a breaking of the attachment. The correct type of partner is shown to be one of an intellectual disposition, a fairly good conversationalist and able to blend interests of a social and public nature with those of a domestic and family character. It is quite possible that the partner will be met whilst you are travelling or as a result of a journey and can be associated with intellectual, educational, newspaper or transport interests.

The number EIGHTEEN shows that as you have a strong desire for domestic comforts there will be a more or less natural attraction towards the condition of marriage and you will be able to do many things yourself towards making marriage a success. At the same time a great deal is shown to depend upon the attitude and activities of the

YOUR LOVE AND MARRIAGE NUMBER 73

partner and there is a possibility of temperamental upsets occurring because the partner either does not, or in certain respects will not, work in with certain of your ambitions, or put forward the same effort as yourself in order to bring about an advancing of material, business, social or public interests. At the same time the partner is shown to have a rather powerful imagination and will be able to extend ideas and to make suggestions that, if applied in a constructive manner, will be productive of mutual benefit. There will, however, be times when the health of the partner will require attention.

The number NINETEEN shows that you will have a strong desire for affection, but signifies that certain of your ambitions can be associated with or influenced by marital conditions and the business, financial and social position of the prospective or actual partner. There will, however, be need for discretion in your choice of partner as an unwise choice could be productive of considerable unhappiness and disappointment. Particular thought should be, in fact, given to the business or social standing of the partner, and it would not be advisable to marry anyone in a lower or mediocre social position as there would be an unfavourable reaction both upon future activities and personal happiness. Finance will also play some part in affairs, and in certain respects can sway your decision regarding the partner. Interests to do with children will have some influence over your decisions.

The number TWENTY in its vibration over marriage shows a strong desire for a home and, therefore, you will want to bring about an attachment that will not last too long before marriage takes place. Hence your best type of partner will naturally be someone who will feel happy in doing cooking and the other domestic features of life, or will be willing to assist in the domestic side. Such a partner will help to bring about a successful marriage. In love affairs before marriage you will find yourself attracted towards the so-called "glamorous types," but as a partner for life this type would not prove suitable for a lasting marriage. After marriage family life is shown to be important, and the reaction of the partner towards the question of children will make or mar the subsequent development of the marriage.

The number TWENTY-ONE, although in many respects a favourable number in its vibration upon love and marriage, follows a kind of two-way path. It intensifies the personal desire for love and affection and will bring the forming of very definite but tense associations. It shows, however, that the individual position in life will have a very strong influence over the actual trend of the love affair and over marriage itself, whilst the position of the prospective or actual partner will also be of very great importance, so much so that it is possible for factors beyond one's own personal control to intervene, even to the extent of denying marriage. You will, therefore, need to take many things into account where love affairs are concerned, and it is possible for a great love to be experienced, and yet also a great sorrow. If marriage is brought about with the loved one, then be prepared to make great sacrifices.

The number TWENTY-TWO is one that will give you quite a broad-minded outlook upon life and consequently upon matters to do with love and marriage. Whilst you will have a natural desire for the companionship of and association with the opposite sex you will try to view things from a practical standpoint and to maintain a practical line of action and hence, if a love affair peters out, as it is quite likely to do, you will try to accept the fact philosophically, even though you will naturally feel hurt. The philosophical acceptance will, however, help to overcome the sting and enable you to bring about another attachment. The number is mainly favourable for marriage and shows that the practical handling of the marital affairs of life will react favourably on marital finances and on the social and kindred interests in which there is a joint operation with the marriage partner.

CHAPTER SIX

YOUR LUCKY AND MONEY NUMBERS

In determining your lucky and money numbers a double sequence of factors has to be employed, for the lucky number can be quite distinct from the number that has rule over the general money indication of your life; but by knowing your lucky number, financial activities can often be arranged in the hour on any particular day that corresponds to your lucky number and thus greater benefit can be derived than would ordinarily be possible.

To find your lucky number you must know the DAY OF THE WEEK on which you were born, whether Sunday, Monday, Tuesday, and so on and the hour of that day on which you were born, The exact minute of the hour does not matter so much. If, for instance, you were born at 6.17 a.m. or p.m. then the hour would count from 6 a.m. or p.m., and so on with other times.

If you were born in 1916 or any year subsequent to that date, and in a part of the world where Single Summer Time or Double Summer Time has been operative, do not forget to allow for the one hour or two hours difference in time. If you were born at say 4.30 a.m. when Single Summer Time was in force, then your correct time of birth would be one hour earlier, *i.e.* 3.30 a.m. and your lucky number would be that number which influenced the hour from 3 to 4 a.m. If you were born when Double Summer Time was in force, say at 8.20 p.m., then your correct time of birth would be *two* hours earlier, *i.e.* at 6.20 p.m. and the number that influenced the hour from 6 to 7 p.m. would be your lucky number.

In the table given on page 78 the hours of each day, from Sunday to Saturday, a.m. and p.m., are given, together with the number that rules the hour. The number shown for your day and hour of birth will be your Lucky Number.

It will be seen that some of the numbers are in bold type and others in ordinary type. Those in bold type show the positive hours and those in ordinary type the negative hours. Naturally, the positive hours strengthen the fortunate vibration and will bring proportionately a great degree of luck than the negative hours, but whichever hour you are born in, positive or negative, the number ruling that hour will be your lucky number.

Once having ascertained your lucky number from the day and hour chart it becomes relatively easy to begin to use its influence for, from the chart, can be seen the hours on the various days of the week when this number is exercising power.

THE SCIENCE OF NUMEROLOGY

BIRTH TIME	SUN. AM	SUN. PM	MON. AM	MON. PM	TUES. AM	TUES. PM	WED. AM	WED. PM	THUR. AM	THUR. PM	FRI. AM	FRI. PM	SAT. AM	SAT. PM
0-1	1	3	7	6	9	8	5	1	3	7	6	9	8	5
1-2	6	9	8	5	4	3	2	6	9	8	5	4	3	2
2-3	5	1	3	7	6	9	8	5	1	3	7	6	9	8
3-4	2	6	9	8	5	4	3	2	6	9	8	5	4	3
4-5	8	5	1	3	7	6	9	8	5	1	3	7	6	9
5-6	3	2	6	9	8	5	4	3	2	6	9	8	5	4
6-7	9	8	5	1	3	7	6	9	8	5	1	3	7	6
7-8	4	3	2	6	9	8	5	4	3	2	6	9	8	5
8-9	6	9	8	5	1	3	7	6	9	8	5	1	3	7
9-10	5	4	3	2	6	9	8	5	4	3	2	6	9	8
10-11	7	6	9	8	5	1	3	7	6	9	8	5	1	3
11-12	8	5	4	3	2	6	9	8	5	4	3	2	6	9

For instance, if you were born on a Monday between 6 and 7 a.m. your lucky number would be 5 and the hours on any other day governed by the number 5 could be used for furthering specific activities, particularly if you could use those hours when a positive 5 is exercising power.

The positive hour or hours would, naturally, be best for anything of an active or constructional nature, but the negative hour or hours ruled by your lucky number would be extremely favourable for studies, research, investigation, etc., and could be used for the filling in of a football coupon or for concentrating upon the result of a horse or dog race, for during these negative hours, the power of inspiration would be considerably stronger than during the positive hours which, as stated, are more for active interests.

To know one's money number, which is completely distinct from one's Lucky Number, we again have to revert to the numerical value of one's name, and in this case the WHOLE of the name, inclusive of Christian or Forenames WITH Surname, must be taken into account. The numbers for each name should be set out separately, then the total of each name added and the final result reduced to 22, or under should it be above 22. The system of the Kabala is used for this and not the Unit system. Once the final number has been obtained, the planetary or zodiacal vibration associated with the number will give the overall indication regarding the general financial fortunes of life.

One or two illustrations of names will be given:—

E D W A R D   W I L L I A M
5 4 6 1 20 4   6 10 12 12 10 1 13
  = 40 = 4   = 64 = 10

        W H I T M A N
        6 8 10 22 13 1 14
             = 74 = 11

The three totals are added: $4+10+11=25=7$.
As the first total came to 25, which is above 22,
the units are added together making the final
number 7. This number will show the overall
financial indications.

All the attributes of the 22 numbers are given
in the following pages of this chapter.

One further illustration of name will be given
so that the principle may be made clear.

G A B R I E L L E   R E N E
3 1 2 20 10 5 12 12 5   20 5 14 5
    = 70 = 7   = 44 = 8

         C A R T E R
         11 1 20 22 5 20
            = 79 = 16

The three totals are added: $7 + 8 + 16 = 31 = 4$.
The final number being 4, that number will
operate over the general money interests of life.

The number ONE in its influence over your
money interests shows that money will be earned
and derived from quite a variety of sources. Some

of these can be of an intellectual and mental nature and others can be connected with travel, transport and certain mechanical affairs, for the influence gives quite a degree of adaptability and it will not take you long to see the possibilities latent in any given condition, to acquire a sufficiency of knowledge to handle it and then to turn it to practical use. Yet you will need to see that you do not fritter away any gain that occurs, or any reserve that you create during the progressive periods, by certain forms of irresponsible or thoughtless expenditure. Particular care will always be required in the making of financial agreements and arrangements and in the signing of financial papers. Never take things too much for granted.

The number Two causes you to have a strong sense of thrift without necessarily being mean. You will not mind spending money, within reason, but you will always do your utmost to obtain full value for the money you do spend. You will invariably do your best to regulate both income and expenditure and this will apply to private as well as to business activities. You will benefit through constructive developments to do with either work or business and through proper attention to details, but there will be occasions when it will be wiser not to express undue criticism of the decisions or actions of others who may be associatedwith your financial interests, for this would only tend to create misunderstanding and unpleasantness and could disturb co-operation or any form of partnership. Additional income could be obtained by using literary ability (if you do not already use this professionally) and by obtaining a knowledge of such things as accountancy, costing, etc., and using this knowledge in a part-time capacity. Sometimes interests to do with food analysis and research and methods of distribution can be made to step up normal income.

The number THREE signifies, in a rather peculiar manner, that you will either gravitate more or less automatically towards interests connected with the financial side of life or they will be drawn to you without any necessarily voluntary action on your part. In either event the use that you make of the opportunities brought by this contact will decide the degree of financial benefit that you ultimately derive. You will have a strong desire for the luxuries and amenities of life but will want money to come easily and without undue personal effort. If this tendency is given way to there will be a danger of yielding to temptations that come into your life and that are brought either by circumstances or by unscrupulous individuals who make suggestions that whilst being attractive are not strictly honest, and if given way to could involve you in transactions of a fraudulent character. Your main weakness will be a reliance upon others, but though this can aid you in obtaining money it will not bring permanent security unless you have a partner or someone to co-operate with who is strictly honest and straightforward.

The number FOUR shows you have the ability to work hard and long in order to obtain money, and with effort you can command quite a good income irrespective of whether you work for yourself or for others. At the same time you will always need to watch expenditure for you will always have an urge to spend money, and unless this is properly controlled you will find yourself taking up obligations and liabilities that will not always be easily redeemed but can be productive of temporary embarrassment. You are not necessarily personally extravagant, but it will be extremely difficult to refrain from spending money on equipment and machinery, especially if you work for yourself, in order to bring about greater efficiency. You will also want certain of the amenities that help to make domestic life more agreeable, but in obtaining these will once again need to use discrimination so as not to overload yourself with payments out. In speculation, forethought will be required and undue risks should not be taken, but you will have quite shrewd judgment respecting investments.

The number FIVE is an exceptionally fortunate number to have as ruler over your financial affairs and shows that you will derive many financial benefits during the course of your life and will experience quite a deal of financial luck and good fortune. Benefit will come through your work and vocational interests, through speculation and investment and quite possibly through legacy or inheritance as well. At the same time there will be occasions when extravagant inclinations will need to be resisted and when unwise risks to do with speculation or investment should be avoided, for should these inclinations be given way to then temporary periods of loss and of financial embarrassment can occur. A great deal will, therefore, depend upon your own handling of affairs. A commonsense approach to all financial matters will ensure progress and a building up of a very substantial reserve, but a taking of affairs too much for granted can interfere with progress and, as stated, bring losses.

The number Six exercises quite a helpful influence over money interests. It creates a vibration of attraction whereby money will come to you, sometimes with but little effort on your part, although this does not imply that you should take things too easily and expect circumstances or luck to bring you everything you desire because if you do you can be sadly mistaken. If, however, proper personal effort is put forth then the fortunate vibration inherent in this planet will help to bring many benefits, both through work and business, and from time to time through speculation and investment. You will also gain through the co-operation of others and through constructive partnership and marriage, providing in the latter instance that a wise choice of partner has been made. On the other hand, should an unwise choice of marriage or business partner have occurred then the danger of loss will be intensified.

The number SEVEN signifies that from a general standpoint money matters will be reasonably progressive and there will be periods of luck and good fortune. Money and income can be derived through a blending of a variety of activities and by combining your main vocational interests with others of a secondary character.

Fluctuations will occur both of income and expenditure and in the latter direction you will need to exercise a degree of commonsense and not rely unduly upon the factor of good luck, for though there will be fortunate periods, you can also experience losses and setbacks through taking certain things too much for granted. On occasions you will benefit through speculation and, in fact, there can be some attraction towards the taking of a risk in the hope of obtaining a substantial gain. You will, however, need to see that this attraction does not become too strong for sometimes your "hunches" will be wrong, and if you take unwise risks then the resulting loss can cause you considerable strain and anxiety and interfere with your progress in other directions of a vocational nature.

The number EIGHT shows that the factor of ambition will be very marked in your life where money is concerned. You will want money both from the standpoint of the security it can give when you have built up a good reserve, as you will invariably do your best to do, and as a means to buy yourself as many of the things you desire, irrespective of whether these are of a domestic or a business nature, or both.

You will always try to regulate expenditure, and on occasions may need to fight against a sense of undue caution which, if allowed to go to an extreme, could stop you from spending money even when it is necessary for you to do so. From a normal standpoint, however, it will be the practical side of your nature which will regulate your activities, showing that you can be careful and yet not necessarily deny yourself of either the necessities or of some of the luxuries of life. You will gain through a developing of business activities and by the holding of responsibilities which link the business and financial sides of life with those of a social, public and political nature, and where you can use your power of organisation.

The number NINE indicates that many of your personal hopes and wishes will be associated with money and with the financial side of life. Alternatively, the obtaining of money and a good income will enable you to bring about a realising of other hopes and wishes connected with the social and public sides of life and with affectional and friendly matters.

Normally, the sign will give much forethought and a deal of practicality in the handling of financial affairs and will strengthen your sense of responsibility in that direction. You will be likely at times during your life to hold positions of trust where other people's money is involved, but should always make a point of seeing that this money never becomes mixed with your own for this could be productive of future upset, misunderstanding and even of loss. You will benefit more as a result of constructive investment than by the taking of speculative risks, for your judgment on the former will be far better than with the latter.

The number TEN signifies that you will have sudden gains and sudden losses, some of which will be caused through unexpected alteration of your vocational activities and others through speculation or the taking of risks. If, however, you let your originality of thought and action aid you, you can derive more gain than loss, particularly if you do your best to plan out affairs ahead and to take proper account of the possible risks and snags that can occur. You will need to watch matters to do with the affections or any form of business partnership or co-operation, for any sudden upset or misunderstanding will react adversely and bring a danger of loss. A maintaining of co-operation will be essential. The number does show a great possibility of gain through such things as sweepstakes, lotteries and football pools.

The number ELEVEN exerts a rather peculiar influence. It gives you the ability to take the long view of affairs, to correctly appraise future possibilities and to use your power of suggestion to influence other people with whom you have financial dealings so that they come round to your line of thought and action and are willing to assist and help you. On the other hand you will always need to guard against trouble or loss through the deception or trickery of others, and at times through dishonesty, actual theft or burglary. There will be occasions when, as a result of encountering difficulties, you will be tempted to do things to overcome the difficulties, that at more normal times would not be contemplated. These temptations should be resisted.

The number TWELVE indicates that, although there will be an experiencing of fluctuations in connection with money matters, from both the income and expenditure standpoints, there will be periods of luck and good fortune as well as a safeguarding of the main financial interests of your life. At the same time it will not be wise to take things too much for granted or to become careless in the handling of money matters as opportunities for deriving benefit could be lost on the one hand and there could be an experiencing of difficulties on the other hand through a neglecting of practical safeguards. Benefit will be derived through a creating of good will and by a proper cultivating of friendly associations as well as through contact with interests of a philosophical, psychic and kindred nature, but there can be loss as a result of imposition, deception and false friends, and through acting too literally upon the suggestions and advice of other people. The inclination to make money easily or quickly should always be resisted, for if this is given way to it can bring contact with dubious characters or a doing of things that, strictly speaking, are not straightforward.

The number THIRTEEN signifies that you will not find it easy to resist the urge to spend money. If this urge is given way to unduly it will cause you to be extravagant and hence will bring times when you will exceed income and in consequence will experience difficulties. Nevertheless, you have capacity to earn money, particularly when you are able to do the work or to give your attention to those things that vitally interest you. In those directions where you experience enthusiasm there will be opportunities to bring about developments that can react very favourably upon money matters. On the other hand, there will be occasions when the inclination to make money quickly or easily will be very pronounced and you will need to be very firm with yourself, resisting tendencies towards speculation or the taking of risks in the hope that you will make big money or at least sufficient to enable you to break away from conditions of work or service that do not appeal to you. Do not let yourself be misled by these tendencies, for they can bring future disillusion. Consistent effort will be necessary if you are to get the income that you desire.

The number FOURTEEN will cause you to be practical in the handling of money matters despite the natural impulse shown by Aries rising. It is quite possible that in some way your work or certain of your personal interests and activities will be associated with money matters and quite a deal of trust will be placed in your integrity and honesty. The acquisitive instinct will be marked, and from a normal standpoint you will endeavour to conserve your financial interests and to build up a reserve. You will usually weigh up the risks you take, especially as regards speculation and investment, but if the end seems to justify the risk then you will go ahead. If you benefit you will use the money gained to strengthen your financial position, but if you should lose, then you will accept the loss in as philosophical a manner as possible and will be guided by the experience gained, in your future transactions.

Benefit can be derived through activities and interests to do with the artistic side of life, such as music, painting, sculpture; and sometimes through entertainment.

The number FIFTEEN denotes that you will derive money and assist normal income as a result of proper planning and a courageous carrying of plans into action. Many of your ideas will be practical, but you will need to be firm and watchful to see that others in higher positions do not usurp them and put them over as their own, thus denying you the rightful proceeds. The accepting of authoritative and responsible positions will aid the financial side of life and, as a result of thrift you will be able to build up quite a substantial reserve. It is a number that is more favourable for investments than for speculation. At times worrying conditions will arise as a result of delays or through your vocational activities being disturbed by national or international difficulties, but your natural forethought will aid you in working through these periods.

The number SIXTEEN, although giving you the capacity to work hard in order to obtain money, shows that though you can obtain a very good income through your own work and efforts, it will not be easy to conserve or to save money because there will always be an urge to spend, and at times an inclination to take risks which you will not be able to control. As a result, money will be lost and obligations will be entered into that will cause quite a deal of future anxiety. In your case much will depend upon whether you are married or not, and upon the manner in which your partner handles money matters. If your partner is practical, then it will be easier for you to restrain extravagance and to save, but if your partner is similar to yourself then financial difficulties will become accentuated from time to time.

The number SEVENTEEN indicates that money and income can be derived from more than one source or through the utilising of more than one kind of activity. Thus, whilst the main source of your income can come from your normal work, business or profession, you can develop an auxiliary source that will give you extra money.

Ability of a literary or kindred nature can be employed, interests to do with transport or travel can have some sway over money matters, or there can be a giving of tuition or instruction to others. Fluctuations of income and expenditure will occur; sometimes things will be very good, but there will be occasions when obligations will compel attention and in doing so will create a temporary sense of apprehension. Yet you will always have plenty of new ideas as to how to draw in money and, though certain of these will not be practical, a lot of them, if knocked into shape, will be productive of benefit. You should, however, always be cautious both in the making and as to the signing of financial agreements, and should be aware of all clauses and conditions before you make the final decision.

The number EIGHTEEN will intensify your power of imagination in regard to money and, in many instances, will influence your decisions in connection with money matters. You will want to attract money to you, and once you acquire it your tenacity in holding it will be very strong, in marked contradistinction to your temperamental restlessness and changeability.

Interests of a domestic and family nature will have some influence over your decisions and actions and it will not always be easy to follow your own inclinations, particularly if you are married, in partnership, or have sons and/or daughters. Nevertheless, their suggestions should always be listened to, as on occasions they will be of value, either in advancing financial interests or in overcoming difficulties. Benefit will come through property, and sometimes through inheritance. On the other hand family upsets, squabbles, disputes can react adversely on overall financial affairs, or demands by the marriage partner or other members of the family can cause personal embarrassment.

The number NINETEEN shows to be very ambitious where money is concerned and will want to do things so as to have a large income, which in turn will enable you to entertain and to take a prominent part in social and public affairs. Fortunately your power of organisation is good and thus will aid you in the handling of people and affairs that are associated with the financial side of your life. There will, however, be times when extravagant inclinations will require restraining and it will not always be easy to exercise this restraint because of a natural desire to have as many of the good things of life as you can.

Unless you do restrain these inclinations you will experience periods when expenditure will exceed income, and as a result, temporary strain and worry will occur until such time as your resourcefulness has enabled you to overcome the difficulties. Speculation and investment will attract you because of the latent possibilities of making money, but it will be essential to maintain practicality and not to lose your sense of proportion. Benefit can be derived, but there are dangers of loss.

The number TWENTY is a helpful number so far as money is concerned, for it draws out personal initiative and enables you to apply personal ability to the acquiring of money. Irrespective of whether your work is mental or manual you will find it relatively easy to adapt your activities to those things from which quite a degree of benefit will be obtained. You will benefit as well through home and family affairs, and this is a number that is often associated with benefit through inheritance or legacy. The constructive planning out of affairs ahead and the maintaining of a practical line of action will always bring you benefit and enable you to create a reserve for future eventualities.

The number TWENTY-ONE is another of the more fortunate numbers and signifies that financial benefits will be derived both through your own initiative and enterprise and as a result of the influence and support of people in influential and authoritative positions who will be well-disposed towards you. In many respects you will have a flair for speculation and investment, although in the former direction a degree of forethought should be exercised and you should not act too much on the spur of the moment. Sometimes matters to do with children and young persons will react very favourably upon overall financial affairs.

The number TWENTY-TWO is a somewhat contrary number in its influence over money. It shows that there will be seasonal fluctuations which can react on your work or your business. On the whole you have a good sense of the value of money, and though you will not mind spending money when you have to you will invariably try to keep a reserve for a rainy day. Conditions of health, both personal and of others in your family, will react upon money interests, and when ill health occurs there will be a loss of income should you be ill yourself, or an incurring of extra expense if someone else is ill.

CHAPTER SEVEN

YOUR NUMBER OF HEALTH

The question of physical strength or weakness is of vital importance to everyone; for upon the maintainance of good health depends, in greater measure than may be commonly realised, the capacity to carry out the daily work and to bring about the developing of plans and activities in all directions of life. Ill health will react upon the earning capacity in many instances, and can disturb or even destroy marital happiness and the continuity of home life. If, therefore, one is aware of one's own peculiar strengths and weaknesses and the liability to certain specific ailments and complaints, one can take the necessary precautions to mitigate the liability to indisposition and to strengthen the general condition of health.

The number of one's name, calculated in accordance with the Kabalistic system of numbers 1 to 22, will again give an unfailing indication of these strengths and weaknesses, and in connection with health two indications are taken.

YOUR NUMBER OF HEALTH 97

The first indication is given by the initial letter and its corresponding number of the FIRST CHRISTIAN OR FORENAME and it can be likened to the indication given by the Rising Sign in an astrological horoscope of birth.

The second indication is once again given by the WHOLE OF THE NAME, Christian and Forenames WITH Surname. The final number given by the whole name will correspond to the planetary or zodiacal vibration which will influence the life generally. As illustrations have been given in earlier chapters on the computation of the number for the name as a whole, there is no need to give a repetition in the present chapter; for once the number has been computed, then the health description given under that number will apply.

To revert, however, to the first indication; that which is given by the Initial Letter of the FIRST Christian or Forename. This is comparatively simple to follow, for all that one does is to take the number allocated to the particular letter which commences the name and then look for the appropriate description of that number.

There is, nevertheless, one distinction which needs to be heeded, and that is, when the first Christian or Forename begins with the letters TH (such as in Thomas) the influence of the TH should be taken in preference to the T by itself, thus bringing in the influence of the number 9 instead of the 22 which normally corresponds to T.

To illustrate:—

With the name EDWARD, the initial letter is E and the corresponding number is 5, therefore, this number gives the first health indication. This, however, will be modified by the health influence of number 4, which is the Kabalistic number of the full Christian name.

We now give the health indications of each number.

The number **1** in its influence over health shows that the general condition of health will be reasonably good so long as you do not give way to mental strain or worry. Directly the latter occurs there will be a reaction on the nerves with a liability to nervous disorders and, should mental tension be permitted to go to an extreme, to nervous breakdowns. On the other hand the maintaining of a cheerful and optimistic outlook on life, which you have undoubtedly the capacity to maintain, will enable you to keep in good health and to enjoy many of the social and pleasurable amenities of life and to do a considerable amount of travel. Travel, especially in country surroundings, will also be an antidote to mental restlessness and anxiety.

The number **2** gives you a neat and fairly compact form of physical body and shows that so long as normal supervision is maintained during the early years of life, good health will result. The sign has rule over the digestive organs and the bowels, chiefly the duodenum, jejunum and ileum, but also the mesentery, peritoneum, spleen and sympathetic nervous system. Any sluggishness of the digestive or eliminative organs should be promptly remedied as otherwise the accumulation of waste matter in the system can be the originating cause of other ailments of a more serious character. Some liability towards suffering from various forms of colic, affections of the intestinal digestion, neuralgia of the intestine, diarrhœa, and the other extreme of constipation, typhoid and enteric fever is denoted. A great deal is shown to depend upon diet as well as upon the climatic and natural conditions of the locality in which you live from time to time. Indisposition can also occur.

The number 3 gives you a well formed and positive type of physical body showing that from a general standpoint health will be good and there will also be good powers of recuperation. At the same time emotional upsets and disturbances will cause a temporary depletion of strength and vitality, almost as severe as a physical illness. The sign has rule over the lumbar region and the skin, the kidneys and supra-renal glands, and, from a structural standpoint the lumbar vertebræ of the spine. There is shown to be some liability to kidney disorders and to complaints affecting or reacting upon the urinary system as well as to ailments caused through an excess of sugar in the system. Any tendency towards jaundice, diabetes, uræmia or kindred complaints should receive immediate attention, whilst there can be some susceptibility to lumbago, gravel and stone. Catarrhal colds affecting the nose and head are denoted.

The number 4 gives you a good deal of physical strength and endurance and shows that good health can be maintained providing normal habits of life are followed. The sign has rule over the pelvis of the kidney, the ureters, bladder, gall, excretory system generally and the pelvic region of the body. Some liability to feverish ailments and those of an internal character is denoted and can affect the parts of the body that have been mentioned. Such complaints as gravel, stone, appendicitis and hernia can occur, whilst there will always be some need for discretion where sexual matters are concerned. Proper precautions should be taken when you are in the vicinity of people suffering from infectious ailments or when passing through localities where there is any form of infection or contagion. As a result of ailments there can be a reaction upon the heart, throat and back.

The number 5 gives a very favourable reaction upon health and shows that, with normal forethought, you will have good health. Even during periods of indisposition there will be compensations and the recuperative powers will pull you through ailments that could prove very disturbing to other people. You will, however, need to be practical where food and drink are concerned. for this number usually gives a very good appetite and hence should you go to excess there could be a building up of fatty tissues and a creating of impurities in the system which would react in the form of boils, abscesses, etc., or in a derangement of the liver. By watching the general condition of the blood and the body these possibilities can, however, be eliminated.

The number 6 again has a very favourable influence over health and assists the general tone of the body and the powers of recuperation. At the same time harmony in the surroundings and agreeable personal relationships, especially of an affectional nature, are essential for the continued preservation of health. When emotional upsets occur or there is a disturbing of associations the subsequent tension will have a reaction almost as bad as an actual physical illness, but with an improvement in these conditions an almost immediate return to a normal condition of health is signified. The condition of the kidneys and of the eyes should be watched.

The number 7 gives you a strong and wiry type of physical body with a good deal of recuperative power, but shows that there will be times when a depletion of health will occur as a result of over activity, over-excitement or through a combination of mental-emotional strain. You should, therefore, always try to regulate periods of work with periods of physical and mental rest, and should control restlessness. The sign has rule over the hips and thighs, the liver, and to some extent the lungs, therefore ailments can affect one or other of these parts of the body. The condition of the blood should always be watched, as any accumulation of impurities therein will manifest in the form of boils, abscesses and local accumulations of waste matter. At certain periods there can be danger of accidents through travel, sports or even through animals. In later years of life it is a sign that brings some tendency to high blood pressure.

The number **8** does not give too strong a type of physical body and shows that health will not be too strong during the earlier years of life, but as it is an earthy sign, there will be a grip upon life, whilst health is shown to improve considerably as age advances. There will be a susceptibility to colds and chills, to complaints of a rheumatic nature and to ailments such as asthma and catarrh. The condition of the digestive and eliminative organs should be watched and any sluggishness should be promptly remedied as otherwise there will be an accumulating of waste matter in the system and consequently greater liability to ill health. The sign has rule over the bones and joints, the knees and kneecap, and the skin. Ailments can, therefore, affect these parts of the body, whilst there is some liability to bruises and to hurt through falls or as a result of things falling upon you.

The number **9** gives you a fairly strong type of physical body, but there is shown to be a need for maintaining purity of the blood and for seeing that there is a proper elimination of carbonic acid gas from the system. Sluggishness of the circulation should not be permitted for this could cause poisoning of the blood stream and create morbid changes unfavourable for health, with an adverse reaction upon the heart. The sign has rule over the legs and ankles, and to some extent the eyes. Any tendency towards varicose veins, affections of the legs or ankles, or hurt to these through accidents or falls, should receive prompt attention. There will be some susceptibility to colds and chills, and you should guard against physical strain and should not lift or carry anything unduly heavy or bulky. Sometimes the sign brings affections of the ears.

The number **10** is another number which signifies that the condition of the nervous system will have much to do with the general health. When there is an absence of mental strain then health will be good, but should affairs deteriorate and cause mental worry or tension then there will be a reaction causing restlessness, loss of sleep, and an upsetting of the digestive organs and stomach. This number also brings a liability to illness as a result of sudden shock or accident, and the latter can be caused through travel, more particularly by road or train, or as a result of taking sudden and unexplained risks in either your daily work or in your hobbies. It is an unfavourable influence for such activities as mountain climbing.

The number **11** is a rather peculiar number and sometimes has a peculiar effect over the health. It is a psychic number and hence gives a receptivity to ailments which are psychic and emotional in their origin. As the imagination is extremely powerful, certain physical aches and pains can be misconstrued and there is a danger of believing that some terrible disease is being suffered when in reality nothing really serious is being experienced. There is, however, some possibility of food poisoning through partaking of tinned or preserved foods, and during periods of illness care will be necessary in the use of drugs. Over-smoking should be avoided.

The number **12** does not give you too strong a type of physical body and there will be some need for guarding against colds and chills affecting the lungs and the respiratory organs generally. At the same time the sign, in an apparently paradoxical manner, is indicative of a good length of life. Therefore, if you take proper precautions when ailments do occur, instead of allowing any form of neglect, you can mitigate the nature of any illness and prevent more serious phases occurring. The condition of the liver and feet should be watched, and cleanliness should be maintained at all times. There will be some need for care in diet, as you will find that certain foods, especially those of a tinned or preserved nature, can have an effect upon you somewhat akin to ptomaine poisoning. The nature of the water you drink, and of other beverages, can react upon the general condition of the health, and water containing an undue residue of lime, sand or chalk would have an unfavourable effect upon the system.

The number **13** gives you a strong type of physical body, good vital powers and plenty of what may be termed life-force. From a general standpoint it signifies that good health will be maintained so long as ordinary thought and care is exercised, but there will be times when you will need to guard against feverish ailments, influenza and illnesses that could affect the head and face. Some liability to hurt through accidents and to cuts and wounds is denoted and these can again affect the head and face. You will find as well that over-activity of either a physical or a mental nature will disturb the health, whilst when indisposition threatens there will be an intensifying of the natural restlessness with a gradually increasing interference with the normally recuperative power of sleep, and if these conditions are permitted to go on indefinitely, insomnia can occur. There will always be some need for guarding against physical strain owing to the tendency to hasty action.

The number **14** gives you a strong type of physical body although there can be some tendency towards stoutness as middle age approaches. Considerable physical endurance is denoted showing a resistance to ill health with a strengthening of the vitality. General good health can be maintained if you avoid going to extremes in any direction and exercise normal discretion regarding food and drink. The latter will be of great importance as usually Taurus is a sign that gives a fairly hearty appetite; therefore, if discretion is not exercised there can be both a clogging of the system with waste matter and a creating of an excess of fat, both of which can have an injurious effect upon the general state of the health. The sign has rule over the throat, neck, ears, eustachian tubes, tonsils, upper part of the œsophagus, vocal cords, cerebellum and the base of the brain, together with the eyes.

The number 15 is not a favourable number for health as it brings a susceptibility to colds and chills, and to illness or malnutrition as a result of neglect—the neglect of others during the earlier years of life, personal neglect during the later years. There will be a liability to hurt through falls or things falling upon you and bones can be broken, especially the bones of the legs. The knee will be a very susceptible part and at times can be affected by rheumatism. Yet in a peculiar manner the number does give a very strong grip upon life and is often associated with a very long life, whilst, if proper care is taken, the latter part of life will be better for health than the first part.

The number **16** gives a strong and muscular type of physical body, and the general health will be good, but there will be a liability to ailments of a feverish nature, particularly if a deal of overseas travel, or residence in hot countries occurs. Some liability to cuts and wounds is signified and can affect the head and face. Care will always be required in the handling of machinery, instruments and knives and anything of an inflammatory nature. It is a masculine number and hence more favourable for men than for women. The inclination towards the taking of risks is accentuated and can lead to accidents.

The number **17** gives you a fairly strong type of physical body but shows that over-activity, either mental or physical, can react upon the health and cause indisposition. The sign has rule over the arms, shoulders and hands, the lungs, breath and blood, whilst from a structural standpoint it governs the clavicle, scapula, humerus, radius, ulna, carpal and metacarpal bones and upper ribs. Some liability to complaints affecting these parts of the body is denoted, such as bronchitis, asthma, pleurisy and other lung troubles, whilst nervous disorders can arise through mental overstrain, and there can be injuries to, or fractures of, the upper limbs as a result of accidents. Mental excitement or any form of undue study or intense mental strain will disturb the health and this can be caused through matters to do with work or with the more private side of life going awry.

The number **18** does not give too strong a type of physical body and there will be a great deal of receptivity to conditions in the surroundings and to matters regarding food and drink, so that health can be disturbed as a result of domestic worries and the stomach and abdominal region of the body can be upset through a wrong diet. At the same time the sign gives an undoubted hold upon life and is indicative of a good length of life. From a general standpoint it has rule over the whole of the chest cavity, the breasts, axillæ, apigastric region, the stomach and abdominal region, whilst from a structural standpoint it governs the sternum, ensiform cartilage and part of the ribs. Ailments can, therefore, affect these various parts of the body causing digestive and gastric troubles, dry coughs affecting the chest and ailments in which there is a preponderance of fluid or phlegm.

The number **19** gives you a strong and well-formed type of physical body and, as it is the strongest physical sign in the zodiac, it is indicative of good health from a general standpoint. It shows, however, that when you are indisposed you can suffer rather severely, although with care the indisposition is usually overcome fairly quickly. The sign has rule over the spine and the back, the heart and blood, and from a structural standpoint the dorsal vertebræ of the spine in particular. Some liability to feverish disorders is shown and complaints can affect the parts of the body that have been mentioned. Undue excitement or over-activity can react on the heart. Treatment of an osteopathic and manipulative nature would prove to be helpful.

The number **20** brings a susceptibility to ailments of a functional nature, and shows that personal cleanliness under all circumstances will be essential for the maintaining of good health. As it rules the stomach and abdominal region of the body, some thought will be required in diet, and pastry concoctions should not be partaken of as they could cause digestive upsets. The breasts and the womb are also under the influence of this number and, with a woman, carelessness can lead to indisposition and to a disturbing of the feminine functions. Yet it is another number that is more helpful during the later years of life and is one often associated with longevity.

The number **21** is a strongly vital number and normally gives extremely good health. It governs the blood and the heart, and warns against any form of activity or over-exertion which could impoverish the blood or react upon the condition of the heart. Sometimes it brings a liability to disorders of an infectious character, but more usually during the younger years of life. Sport in moderation will help to preserve good health and the natural strength is shown to continue until well into the 60's, but after 65 natural precautions should certainly be maintained and, despite the feeling of robustness, risks should not be taken.

The number **22** shows that the season of the year during which you were born will have a great deal to do with the general condition of health. If you were born in the Spring there will be a need for regulating over-activity and for controlling both physical and mental restlessness. If you were born in the Summer your vitality is good but outbursts of temper could be injurious. If born in the Autumn much will depend upon your associations with others and your marital life. If happy, health will be good, but if unhappy or disturbed, then health will be upset. If you were born in the Winter you will need to guard against colds and should always keep warm. Health will not be strong during the first part of life but will strengthen as age increases.

CHAPTER EIGHT

COLOUR AND NUMBERS

In the same way as each number from 1 to 22 has its specific influence over character, luck, money, marriage and health, so it has rule over a particular colour, and the colour shown by your PERSONAL NUMBER, that is the number derived from your Christian name or names, will indicate your lucky colour and you should do your best to wear this colour from time to time, or to wear a stone or gem of this colour, or in which this colour predominates.

Naturally with women it will be easier to wear clothes in which the lucky colour is prominent; but even with men it should not be too difficult to find a shirt, a tie or even socks in which the lucky colour is predominant.

The number ONE rules the colour Yellow, and the wearing of this colour will help to draw out the powers of intuition and inner wisdom.

The number TWO has as its colour Dark Blue striped with White. Its wearing will assist the capacity for study, research and investigation. It is very good for occult studies.

The number THREE rules Light Blue, and in wearing this colour there will be an intensifying of the powers of reasonableness and of goodness. It is helpful for activities of a social and public nature.

The number FOUR governs Dark Red, and though care is shown to be required in the wearing of this colour owing to its intensity and its tendency to excite the feelings and emotions and to cause precipitate action, if this number is your Personal Number, then the wearing of Red will draw out courage, initiative and enterprise, and so long as commonsense is maintained will aid you in the furthering of your desires and ambitions.

The number FIVE has rule over the colour Violet, and its use in dress or by wearing a precious stone of this colour will draw out your love of truth, will cause you to be responsive to religious and philosophical urges and will give earnestness of spirit. It accentuates the vibration of Luck.

The number SIX governs the colour Blue in its entirety and shows that varying shades, from light to dark, can be worn. It will draw out the companionable side of the nature and will aid matters to do with the affections, marriage and partnership.

The number SEVEN brings a composite colour of Yellow and Brown. Its wearing will aid the intellectual powers and the practical carrying into operation of thoughts and ideas.

The number EIGHT rules Grey, and this is another colour the use of which will assist the power of concentration and of organisation, and is helpful when there are business or working interests to be dealt with.

The number NINE governs Dark Brown or Dark Blue streaked with white, and by wearing it the factor of hope will be intensified, while it aids the focusing of thought when there is need for the expressing of knowledge.

The number TEN rules all kinds of Check and Tartan colours, Black and White, Brown and White and combinations of other colours, and by wearing one of these various blends the originality of thought and action will be accentuated and it will be easier to reach decisions of importance.

The number ELEVEN has power over the colour Mauve, and it is another colour whose wearing will draw out the spiritual and the psychic sides of the nature. It will assist in the developing of certain psychic powers such as clairvoyance, psychometry, etc.

The number TWELVE rules dazzling White. It is a colour symbolizing purity, and by wearing it there will be a drawing out of the inner virtues and it will help to create more restful conditions and to overcome changeability.

The number THIRTEEN governs Light Red. Its use enhances the active, enterprising and pioneering side of the nature, and once again draws out personal courage. It is good for using with sporting interests.

The number FOURTEEN is another number associated with the darker shades of Blue and sometimes with Russet, and the wearing of either of these colours will aid the powers of perception whilst the Russet will seem to intensify the capacity to express criticism when it is considered necessary.

The number FIFTEEN rules the colour Black, and its use, whilst being very appropriate for ceremonial occasions and for evening dress, will help to accentuate the natural dignity and bearing of the wearer and will subconsciously compel the attention of others.

The number SIXTEEN is another number associated with Red, but with the brilliant and intense shades of red bordering on to Crimson. Care will be required in its use as it is a dramatic colour, but it can very well be used if one takes part in theatrical and kindred affairs.

The number SEVENTEEN governs the Greenish-Yellow colour. By wearing it the capacity for adaptability will be intensified and in certain instances it will seem to exercise a power that will bring about quite a degree of travel.

The number EIGHTEEN rules the colour Green, and by using it there will be a strengthening of sympathy, of the "mother spirit" and of aspiration. It will aid all matters to do with the home and domestic side of life.

The number NINETEEN governs the colour Gold. Its use will intensify the natural pride, will give a good physical bearing and assist the powers of vitality and recuperation.

The number TWENTY-ONE rules the colour Orange, and this is another spiritual colour and one that will draw out the artistic side of the nature.

The number TWENTY governs the colour Silver, and is another number and colour associated with formal and ceremonial occasions, especially if one wishes to draw the attention of others.

The number TWENTY-TWO governs pale Greenish Blue, and the wearing of this colour is favourable for bringing about a blending of domestic with social activities, and for creating harmony.

CHAPTER NINE

NUMBERS AND SPECULATION

The following chapter is written essentially from the point of view of the resident in Great Britain, although the principles expounded through Numerology can be used throughout in any similar way in any country of the world, provided one has the necessary local knowledge. They have greyhound racing tracks in Chicago similar to those in London. The dogs race out of traps numbered 1—6, and if the combination of lucky numbers succeeds in London, it could be equally successful in Chicago—or in any other place in the world.

In some measure the numbers forecast concerning the winning teams in Football can be made in any country where Football is played and fostered, for the purpose of gambling for capital gains.

Any information concerning Stock and Share transactions can be used by anyone interested since a large proportion of Securities quoted on the Stock Exchanges can be traded in other parts of the world.

Football Pools

Although infallibility is not claimed, it should be possible to work out a system of forecasting for football pools by the use of numbers. The name of each team obviously has a numerical value, and if the teams playing each other possess the same value, then the possibility should be toward a draw; if, however, the two numbers differ attention should be paid to whether the numbers are positive or negative. The positive numbers, as a rule being the stronger, should add to the team's chances. A further check can be made by working out the number of the date on which the match is played—*e.g.* 23/1/1958. By adding the units of this date together we have a total 29 which, reduced to 22 or under in accord with the Kabalistic system, reduces to 11. All odd numbers are positive and even numbers negative.

For the convenience of readers we append below a list of all the football teams together with their individual numbers, taking first the total number and then the reduced number, again in terms of the Kabala. The names have been taken according to popular use.

LIST OF FOOTBALL TEAMS SHOWING NUMBERS

	Total	Reduces To		Total	Reduces To
Arsenal	74	11	Airdrie	70	7
Aston Villa ...	115	7	Albion	55	10
Aldershot ...	109	10	Alloa	42	6
Accrington ...	122	5	Arbroath ...	90	9
Aberdeen ...	56	11	Ayr United ...	92	11

THE SCIENCE OF NUMEROLOGY

	Total	Reduces To		Total	Reduces To
Bolton	82	10	Doncaster ...	114	6
Blackpool ...	98	17	Derby	41	5
Burnley	69	15	Darlington ...	116	8
Birmingham ...	94	13	Dumbarton ...	98	17
Bristol Rovers	191	11	Dunfermline...	120	3
Bristol City ...	156	12	Dundee... ...	38	11
Bury	38	11	Dundee United	99	18
Barnsley ...	85	13	Everton ...	88	16
Berwick R. ...	151	7	Exeter	72	9
Blackburn ...	79	16	East Fife ...	98	17
Brentford ...	120	3	E. Stirling ...	161	8
Brighton ...	95	14	Fulham ...	57	12
Bournemouth	128	11	Falkirk	82	10
Bradford ...	84	12	Forfar	91	10
Bradford City	137	11	Grimsby ...	79	16
Barrow	65	11	Gillingham ...	86	14
Brechin City...	123	6	Gateshead ...	70	7
Cardiff	80	8	Huddersfield...	116	8
Charlton ...	104	5	Halifax	64	10
Chelsea	63	9	Hull	38	11
Colchester ...	131	5	Hartlepools ...	150	6
Coventry ...	104	5	Hamilton ...	96	15
Crystal Palace	144	9	Hearts	77	14
Carlisle	92	11	Hibernian ...	84	12
Crewe	47	11	Ipswich... ...	83	11
Chesterfield ...	140	5	Kilmarnock ...	119	11
Chester	92	11	Leeds	47	11
Celtic	71	8	Luton	70	7
Clyde	42	6	Leicester ...	111	3
Cowdenbeath	94	13	Leyton Orient	166	13

NUMBERS AND SPECULATION

	Total	Reduces To		Total	Reduces To
Lincoln	89	17	Rangers ...	84	12
Liverpool ...	114	6	Sunderland ...	101	2
Manchester U'd	181	10	Sheffield W.	169	16
Man. City ...	173	11	Southport ...	148	13
Middlesboro'	124	7	Stoke	75	12
Millwall... ...	78	15	Sheffield United	160	7
Mansfield ...	97	16	Swansea ...	69	15
Motherwell ...	119	11	Shrewsbury ...	119	11
Montrose ...	127	10	Southend ...	96	15
Morton	101	2	Southampton	156	12
Newcastle ...	97	16	Swindon ...	85	13
Notts. County	174	12	Scunthorpe ...	140	5
Nott'm Forest	224	8	Stockport ...	156	12
Newport ...	100	1	Stenhousemuir	167	14
Northampton	163	10	St. Johnston...	164	11
Norwich ...	85	13	St. Mirren ...	125	8
Oldham ...	54	9	Stirling Albion	167	14
Portsmouth ...	161	8	Stranraer ...	124	7
Preston	115	7	Tottenham H.	233	8
Port Vale ...	99	18	Torquay ...	94	13
Plymouth ...	104	5	Tranmere ...	100	1
Partick	92	11	Third Lanark	125	8
Q.P. Rangers	203	5	West Bromwich	140	5
Queens Park...	119	11	West Ham ...	76	13
Queen of the South ...	190	10	Watford ...	86	14
			Walsall	65	11
Rotherham ...	113	5	Wolverhampton	156	12
Reading... ...	57	12	Workington ...	132	6
Rochdale ...	77	14	Wrexham ...	68	14
Raith Rovers	149	14	York	57	12

In order to assist the making of a decision regarding the relative numerical strength of either team involved in a match, the number ruling the hour in which the match commences can also be taken into account. (The hour numerical values are given on page 78, Chapter Six.)

In addition, the number ruling the day, and the number ruling the town in which the match is played have to be allowed for. The number ruling the town should be computed in the same way as for a person's name, the number of each letter being taken—from 1 to 22—and then added to obtain the grand total, and from this the reduced total.

The numbers of the days of the week are as follows:

Sunday, 1 and 4; Monday, 2 and 7; Tuesday, 9; Wednesday, 5; Thursday, 3; Friday, 6; Saturday, 8

To the number of the team should be added the number of the day, the number of the hour, the reduced number of the place where the match is played. The total number obtained should again be reduced to 22 or under should it exceed 22, and this final number will show the possibility of success or loss along the lines suggested in the opening paragraph of this chapter.

Stocks and Shares

In order to use numbers to forecast the rise and fall of stocks and shares a slightly different system is required. This system calls for a certain knowledge of planetary influence over stocks, together with the vibration of the basic number ruling the name of any given undertaking. For instance, Imperial Tobacco, the total of which is 167 reducing to 14 and then to 5 (in this system every number is reduced to a unit) is a negative Sun number and Tobacco is ruled by the planet Venus. Reference must of necessity be made to the current ephemeris to discover when there are good or bad aspects by the Sun or other planets to Venus, as these will show the trend, good aspects indicating rises and the bad forewarning falls. So far as the Sun and Venus are concerned, the Sun can only make three aspects to Venus—*i.e.* conjunction (good); semi-sextile (slightly good) and semi-square (slightly bad). Venus itself, however, can make good and bad aspects to the other planets during the course of the year.

We append below a list of the planets and the undertakings which they govern.

SUN: All Government stocks; precious stones and metals (except silver) and Diamonds.

MOON: Silver; waterboards; soft drinks; land and property.

MERCURY: Steam railways; newspapers; road

transport; Municipal and Corporation stock; plastics; printing.

VENUS: Banks; tobacco; diamonds; copper; money exchange; amusements.

MARS: Iron and steel; motors and engineering; beer and spirits; armaments; rubber.

JUPITER: Overseas shares; shipping; insurance; paper and publishing.

SATURN: Coal; bricks and cement; building materials; industrials.

URANUS: Electrical; air, scientific, atomic and nuclear interests.

NEPTUNE: Oils; drugs.

In making a personal decision as to the taking up of certain types of shares one can be reasonably assured of deriving benefit by taking shares that are associated with one's Lucky and Money number as described in Chapter Six, and these can be classified briefly as follows:

Number 1: Transport, railways, newspapers, aluminium, printing machinery, making of type, accessories, etc.

Number 2: Industrial shares such as tea, coffee, cocoa, cereals, catering and food stores, bazaars, etc.; restaurants.

Number 3: Diamonds, luxury goods generally, watches and clocks, perfumes, high class, hairdressing and kindred establishments, furs.

Number 4: Chemicals, drugs, dyes, laundries and all interests of a sanitary nature, rubbers breweries, wines, spirits, hotels, surgical instrument makers.

Number 5: Shipping, overseas shares, tin, publishing, periodicals, law stationers, makers of wigs, gowns, etc.

Number 6: Copper, currency exchange, tobacco, entertainments and amusements, art and commercial art, precious stones.

Number 7: Insurance, shipping, tin, paper making.

Number 8: Government securities, mines generally, coal specifically, bricks, cement and building materials.

Number 9: Aircraft, musical publishing, making of musical instruments, making of gymnastic apparatus, television, cables.

Number 10: Making of scientific instruments, atomic, nuclear and kindred interests; electricity, refrigerators, vacuum cleaners, etc.

Number 11: Psychic publications, making of psychic apparatus, crystals, etc.; drugs, preservatives, anæsthetics, oils.

Number 12: All requisites to do with hospitals and nursing homes, such as bandages, beds. hospital furniture, invalid chairs; all shares that cater for fishing interests, film production, cinema shares.

Number 13: Wool and woollen products, timber, iron and steel manufacturing interests (not iron mines), construction and demolition shares, armaments.

Number 14: Banks, financial trusts, leather, cattle, tobacco, dental interests, optical interests (glasses, binoculars, telescopes, etc.).

Number 15: Coal mines and coal producing machinery, pit props and pit head gear; slate, concrete and building materials, government stock.

Number 16: Iron and steel shares, iron mines, cutlery, all shares to do with road and bridge making and building.

Number 17: Newspapers, radio, telephony, road transport, steam railways, municipal and corporation stock.

Number 18: Water board shares, soft drinks industry, property and land shares, agriculture, farming and dairy farming, milk, antiques,

Number 19: Sporting interests—boxing, football, cricket, lawn tennis, etc.; educational matters, theatrical interests.

Number 20: Property, silver, furniture, interior decorations and furnishings; all domestic appliances, water softeners, detergents, soaps.

Number 21: Gold, theatrical and sporting shares, gilt-edged stocks, entertainments and records.

Number 22: Industrial shares, agriculture, land, forestry, motors and engineering, weather resisting clothes and apparatus.

Some of the numbers overlap with others so far as certain shares are concerned, but as broad an outline as possible has been given.

In the buying of stocks and shares one can, of course, do so during the hours of the day when one's lucky and money number are operative, as shown in the table on page 78, Chapter Six, particularly if one does not understand astrology; and this is really the simpler method. Better results will naturally be obtained if one can buy or sell during the positive hours.

Horse and Greyhound Racing

The use of numbers can be applied to horse and greyhound racing in a somewhat similar manner as that already described for the choosing of the prospective winner in a football match.

The factors employed are (*a*) the name of the horse or greyhound reduced to number 9 or under by the addition of the numbers corresponding to the letters of the name and their subsequent reduction; (*b*) the reduced number of the name of the place where the race is run; (*c*) the number of the day of the race; and (*d*) the number of the hour in which the race is run.

When these four numbers have been obtained they should again be added together and the total reduced to number 9 or under by the addition of the units of the total number.

The winning numbers for horse races are: 1, 3, 5, 7, 9. The losing numbers are: 2, 4, 6, 8.

If the combination of numbers of any horse reaches a reduced total of 2, 4, 6 or 8, that horse can be eliminated.

When the reduced total reaches 1, 3, 5, 7 or 9, then again a process of elimination must be employed in order to see which horses have the best chances of winning.

If the reduced total is in accord with the number ruling the hour in which the race is run, then the horse which that reduced total signifies stands the best opportunity of winning the race; with the proviso that, if the hour in which the race is run happens to be ruled by one of the negative or losing numbers of 2, 4, 6 or 8, then the positive equivalents of these numbers must always be substituted, as under:—

For negative 2 substitute positive 7
,, ,, 4 ,, ,, 1
,, ,, 6 ,, ,, 3
,, ,, 8 ,, ,, 9.

As a final factor in selection of horses, the colours worn by the jockeys can be taken into account, and the number as shown by the main colour (see Chapter 8 for colours and their respective numbers) if corresponding with the reduced number value of the horse in question, will often help to point to the winner; or, from the standpoint of experimentation, the number of the colour could also be added to the other numbers and yet a fresh reduced total obtained. An interesting sequence of number factors could thus be obtained and, as a result of experience, the more relevant used.

With greyhound racing there is also a need for

a substitution of certain numbers, for only six dogs at the most take part in these races and, therefore, the numbers from 1 to 6 only can be employed.

When the reduced total of all the factors involved: dog's name, place of race, number of day and number of hour, reaches a 7 it will convert to two; if it reaches 8 it will convert to one; if it reaches 9 it will convert to five.

This conversion is different from the conversion for the numbers of the hours and should not be confused therewith. The converted numbers in this respect have no relation to the trap number in which the dog is placed. It is the *name* of the dog, with the other factors, that is employed.

Nevertheless, if desired, the trap number could be added to the other numbers and the selection based upon the reduced total so found; but in this case there would naturally be an alteration, and the winning and losing numbers, as given for horse races, would not apply.

The method of selection in this case would be that the reduced number should coincide with the number of the hour in which the race is run.

As an added refinement, one could also take the sub-period number of the hour into account; for each hour of 60 minutes can be sub-divided into 15 periods of four minutes, and the sub-period number for the exact time of the start of the race would then prove to be the more favoured number.

A table of sub-period numbers for each of the

hour numbers from 1 to 9 is appended, but do not forget to convert a 7 to 2, an 8 to 1, and a 9 to 5, remembering that for greyhound races only the numbers from 1 to 6 can be employed.

SUB-PERIOD TABLE
HOUR NUMBERS

TIME IN MINUTES	1	2	3	4	5	6	7	8	9
0—4	**1**	2	3	4	**5**	6	**7**	8	**9**
5—8	6	**8**	**9**	**6**	2	**5**	8	**3**	4
9—12	**5**	**3**	**1**	5	**8**	2	**3**	**9**	**6**
13—16	2	**9**	6	**7**	3	**8**	9	**1**	5
17—20	**8**	4	**5**	8	**9**	3	**1**	6	**7**
21—24	3	**6**	2	**3**	4	**9**	6	**5**	8
25—28	**9**	5	**8**	9	**6**	4	**5**	2	**3**
29—32	4	**7**	3	**1**	5	**6**	2	**8**	9
33—36	6	**8**	**9**	6	**7**	5	**8**	3	**1**
37—40	5	**3**	4	5	8	**7**	3	**9**	6
41—44	**7**	9	**6**	2	**3**	8	**9**	4	**5**
45—48	8	**1**	5	8	9	**3**	4	**6**	2
49—52	**3**	6	**7**	3	**1**	9	**6**	5	**8**
53—56	9	**5**	8	9	6	**1**	5	**7**	3
57—60	**1**	2	**3**	4	**5**	6	**7**	8	**9**

Bold type numbers are positive sub-period numbers and ordinary type numbers are negative sub-period numbers